SOFT TISSUE INJURIES & HARDBALL TACTICS

(Dealing with Soft Tissue Injuries and Insurance Companies)

By: William J. ("B.J.") Kelley II
© 2013

Craig, Kelley & Faultless
5845 Lawton Loop East Drive
Indianapolis, Indiana 46216

and

1305 Tekulve Road
Batesville, Indiana 47006
1-800-746-0226
www.ckflaw.com

AUTHOR BIOGRAPHICAL INFORMATION

William J. Kelley II (B. J.) grew up in southeastern Indiana. He graduated from Emory University in 1981 and Georgetown University Law School with honors (cum laude) in 1985. During law school, he was accepted into the American Criminal Law Review and was also a member of DC Law Students in Court where he helped local citizens and tried his first cases while still in law school.

After graduating from law school, he was admitted into the Attorney General's Honors Program, which, according to the Department of Justice, is "the most prestigious federal entry-level attorney hiring program of its kind." During his time as a trial lawyer with the Justice Department, he handled cases and trials in federal courts all across the United States.

In 1992, after spending ten years in Washington, DC, B. J. and his wife Lisa (a pediatrician) moved back to the Hoosier state to raise their two children. For twenty years, B. J. has devoted his legal career to representing injured people. During that time, he estimates that he has personally negotiated and resolved more than five thousand personal injury cases. He has also participated in jury trials in various Indiana and Ohio courts and has spoken at legal and medical seminars.

B. J. has a special interest in the medical side of the firm's cases and has worked with numerous doctors and medical specialists over the years to ensure that Craig, Kelley & Faultless can provide insurance companies and juries with the best information possible regarding their clients' injuries and treatment.

B. J. is a Top 100 trial lawyer according to the National Trial Lawyers and a Top 100 litigator According to the American Society of Legal Advocates. He is admitted to practice in Pennsylvania, the District of Columbia, Indiana, and Ohio.

TABLE OF CONTENTS

I. INTRODUCTION

I am an attorney who has been practicing law for over twenty-seven years. For the last twenty years, I have focused my practice entirely on representing injured people. The vast majority of the cases handled by my firm, Craig, Kelley & Faultless, involve auto, semi, and motor-cycle wrecks. Our overriding goal is to help the people who have been injured in these wrecks.

During my career, I have resolved thousands of soft tissue injury cases—either by settlement, arbitration, or trial. For purposes of this book, "soft tissue injury" means injuries to muscles, tendons, and liga-ments. These injuries do not involve broken bones, lacerations, brain injuries, or spinal disc injuries. The subtitle of this book could be "sprains, strains, and automobiles,"[1] because that's probably ninety percent of what we are talking about—injuries that start off as sprains and strains to the neck and back from automobile wrecks. But, unlike a simple ankle sprain, soft tissue injuries from wrecks sometimes don't resolve on their own within a week or two. When the recovery becomes more compli-cated, the insurance companies become much more difficult to deal with.

Many people who incur these injuries simply believe they are just "a little sore" and will get better in a few days. They often don't con-tact lawyers because they believe there is no need. Those who do not recover quickly, often continue to wait in the hope that one day they will miraculously wake up to a full recovery. Eventually, when the mira-cle fails to materialize, they may seek some sort of treatment and begin dealing with the insurance carrier for the driver who caused the wreck. At this point, the injured person has moved into the cross hairs of the insurance industry. They are at the mercy of experienced adjusters who have one overriding goal—to minimize the claim. These adjusters will use any tactic they believe will accomplish their goal, regardless of the effect the tactic has on the injured person.

---

1 I cannot claim to have originated this phrase. I believe that at some point I saw a seminar with this title. Also, a quick Internet search revealed a book by the same title. However, the lead author is employed in the insurance industry: http://www.carswell.com/product-detail/sprains-strains-and-automobiles-a-medically-illustrated-guide-to-commonly-litigated-injuries/.

The information contained in this book is designed to: A) inform and help people who have been injured in wrecks; B) be of assistance to attorneys who may want to give the book to clients to help them understand the claim process; C) be of assistance to attorneys who may want to use the book as a simple reference with cites to current information on soft tissue injury claims; and D) inform the general public about how insurance carriers and attorneys handle soft tissue injury claims. The book is *not* designed as a "how to" manual for experienced personal injury lawyers.

This book has been written from my perspective as an advocate for the average citizen who, after a wreck, is being squeezed, pushed, and prodded by large corporate forces beyond his or her control. The book explains why the insurance carrier will, at some point in the claim process, employ hardball tactics to force that person in the direction the carrier desires.

I make my living by intervening in these cases, helping injured people manage their claims, and forcing the insurance companies to honor their contracts. I am paid a portion of the final result that I obtain from the insurance carriers. My pay is based solely on performance. The more the insurance companies pay, the more money I make. You could say that I am biased, and you might be right. However, my partners and I have made a living by promoting fairness, equity, and honesty. We present our cases, whether in settlement discussions or jury trials, in the most straightforward way possible. I have tried to do the same in this book.

Although I have never represented an insurance company, I do not consider this book to be "anti-insurance." Instead, it is brutally honest and based on facts and innumerable personal experiences.

Finally, while I fight for my clients with every ounce of energy and determination I can muster, I still maintain cordial relationships with a large number of insurance adjusters and claims supervisors, many of whom are simply carrying out the marching orders formulated by corporate higher-ups. I believe that if you asked, many of these folks would tell you that they respect my firm's integrity even though they are not always permitted to agree with the value we place on our clients' claims.

II. WHAT INSURANCE COMPANIES DO—AND DON'T DO—WHEN YOU'VE BEEN IN A WRECK

A. What Insurance Companies Don't Do

Insurance companies do not exist to be your "good neighbor," to hold you in their "good hands," or to be "on your side." Dealing with them will not make you "as happy as an antelope with night vision goggles." Nor will you generally find the injury claims process to be "so easy a caveman can do it"; although, after a while, you may feel like hitting someone with a club!

Let's be absolutely clear—in today's world, if you've been injured in a wreck that was caused by someone else, their insurance company is not interested in providing you with assistance and making sure you are treated fairly. In fact, your interests and their interests are the exact opposite of one another.

I tell our clients that *insurance companies make money by taking in as much as they can in premiums, investing that money for as long as possible and paying out as little as they possibly can in claims.* That's the insurance business. All of those warm-hearted and clever TV commercials are just that—TV commercials.

Not only do insurance companies make money by taking in as much as possible and paying out as little as possible, they also make significant sums investing the premium money they take in before they have to pay it out. That money is called the "float." In fact, carriers often take in less in premiums than they pay out in claims and still make huge overall profits from their investments. As mega-billionaire Warren Buffet (whose company owns a large portion of GEICO) once said about the miracle of float, it's "money we hold that is not ours but which we get to invest."[1] And that investment income adds up to serious money. State Farm "is among the top five shareholders of International Business Machines (IBM), Johnson & Johnson (JNJ), and Caterpiller, Inc. (CAT), with holdings *in each* of more

---

1 *Delay, Deny, Defend;* Jay M. Feinman, Portfolio (2010), p. 16, from Warren Buffett, 2006 Berkshire Hathaway Inc. Shareholder Letter, www.berkshirehathaway.com/letters/2006ltr.pdf.

than $2 billion . . ."[2] In his book, *Delay, Deny, Defend,* Jay Feinman found that "in 2007 [insurance] industry investment profits totaled 58 billion."[3]

Insurance in the United States has come a long way from its 18th Century origins. Back then, groups of property owners got together and paid sums of money into a fund to protect themselves against the risk of fire (a very real risk in the days when most homes were built of wood and neighborhood fires were fought with "bucket brigades").[4] These companies were operated on a cooperative basis. The policyholders in these groups all had a common interest—to help those who had suffered a loss. "Because these companies were formed by businesses and individuals to share losses, they were keenly aware of their responsibility to pay claims."[5] Not so these days. Today's insurance companies are large, impersonal businesses driven by the desire to squeeze out extra dollars from the claims process, drive corporate value and stock prices ever upward, and fund lavish salaries for millionaire executives.

If you have a soft tissue injury from a wreck that was not your fault, you are EXACTLY in the middle of the insurance industry's crosshairs and you are about to be squeezed...in a most uncomfortable way. And, the tactics they will use against you will make it exceptionally difficult for you to fight them alone.

1. Claims Handling Changes in the Last 20 Years

Over the last 20 years, insurance carriers have drastically changed the way they handle claims, especially soft tissue injury claims. The two largest auto insurers, State Farm and Allstate, led the way. The other companies then followed suit.

Insurance is not like most other corporate endeavors. Insurance carriers are regulated by the states in ways that are similar to public utili-

---

2 "State Farm Profit Plunges 56% on 2011 Natural Disasters," by Andrea Ludtke, *The Huffington Post* (March 1, 2012), http://www.bloomberg.com/news/print/2012-03-01/state-farm-annual-profit-declines-56-to-800-million-on-natural-disasters.html.

3 *Delay, Deny, Defend;* Jay M. Feinman, Portfolio (2010), p. 16.

4 See *Delay, Deny, Defend;* Jay M. Feinman, Portfolio (2010), pp. 13–14.

5 *Delay, Deny, Defend;* Jay M. Feinman, Portfolio (2010), pp. 13–14.

ties. The premium money insurance companies hold does not technically belong to them (i.e., the "float" discussed earlier), and carriers are bound by a duty of good faith in many instances. Consequently, the claims handling changes carriers have made over the last 20 years are more than simple changes in philosophy and procedure. Instead, many carriers have intentionally put in place claims handling procedures that are designed to push the envelope (and in many cases exceed the envelope) of legality.

In 1992, Allstate hired the well-known consulting firm McKinsey & Company (the same consulting firm that helped engineer Enron's "success") to redesign its business model so that more dollars could be wrung out of the claims department. Instead of promoting service and assistance to customers and claimants who had suffered a loss, claims became a profit-driven portion of the business relying on bogus computer programs that spit out intentionally low settlement offers.[6] Interestingly, the biggest targeted group of cases were not the biggest dollar value cases, but rather the group of cases that comprised the biggest (by far) number of claims. *Allstate, and virtually every other carrier, soon focused their sights on soft tissue injury claims.*

As Jay Feinman said in a December 2011 interview with the *Huffington Post*, "[an] insurance company can make a lot of money on the small claims because if you save a few dollars on a huge number of claims, it's worth more than saving a lot of dollars on a very small number of claims."[7] And "Allstate has certainly gained: It made $4.6 billion in profits in 2007, double its earnings in the 1990s. The stunning increase, said Russ Roberts, came through 'driving down loss values to an average of 30 percent below the actual market cost'—that is, paying dramatically less on claims."[8] As a result of this fine work, Allstate CEO Tom Wilson made $9.3 million in 2010, while thousands of loss victims

6 See generally *From Good Hands to Boxing Gloves*, by David Berardinelli, Trial Guides LLC (2006, 2008); see also http://www.huffingtonpost.com/2011/12/13/insurance-claim-delays-industry-profits-allstate-mckinsey-company_n_1139102.html.

7 http://www.huffingtonpost.com/2011/12/13/insurance-claim-delays-industry-profits-allstate-mckinsey-company_n_1139102.html.

8 http://www.huffingtonpost.com/2011/12/13/insurance-claim-delays-industry-profits-allstate-mckinsey-company_n_1139102.html. Emphasis added.

were grossly undercompensated.[9] In 2011, State Farm CEO Ed Rust's base compensation *decreased* 9.3% to $9.25 million.[10]

2. <u>Big Money = Big Incentives</u>

Those are obviously very large salaries and would provide these CEOs with considerable motivation to keep profits as high as possible, especially if their pay is tied to the company's performance. However, those numbers are dwarfed by the real dollar amounts at stake for these executives. According to Allstate's 2005 proxy, the CEO is required to own (within five years of the date the executive position is assumed) Allstate stock worth *seven times the base salary*.[11] That requirement would mean that, by now, Mr. Wilson must own Allstate stock worth approximately $65.1 million, which gives him a rather large incentive to keep stock prices as high as possible. If his performance were tied, instead, to claims satisfaction, I probably would not be writing this book.

However, the real pot at the end of the rainbow for these executives may be yet to come. In *From Good Hands to Boxing Gloves,* David Berardinelli pointed out the following about Allstate's prior CEO, Ed Liddy,

> At the time of his retirement on December 31, 2006, Liddy owned 3,823,255 shares of Allstate stock, worth approximately $250,000,000 at a market price of $65.11. This is in addition to about $20 million he received for selling some of his Allstate stock between August 2004 and August 2005, and another $16 million from his sale of Allstate stock in 2006.
>
> On top of this, Allstate's 2007 proxy statement reports that on December 31, 2006, Liddy received approximately $50 million in 'Amounts Immediately Payable Upon Effective date of

---

9   http://www.huffingtonpost.com/2011/12/13/insurance-claim-delays-industry-profits-allstate-mckinsey-company_n_1139102.html.

10   "State Farm Profit Plunges 56% on 2011 Natural Disasters," by Andrea Ludtke, *The Huffington Post* (March 1, 2012), http://www.bloomberg.com/news/print/2012-03-01/state-farm-annual-profit-declines-56-to-800-million-on-natural-disasters.html. The decrease was due to company losses as a result of multiple natural disasters.

11   *From Good Hands to Boxing Gloves*, by David Berardinelli, Trial Guides LLC (2006, 2008), p. 61.

Change-in-Control. Last, but hardly least, Allstate's 2007 Proxy Statement states that in four years Liddy will receive his retirement package, which looks to be worth roughly $71 million.

In all, Liddy's move to Allstate in 1994 netted a personal fortune of approximately $350 million upon his retirement on December 31, 2006—much of it due directly to McKinsey's business model.[12]

And even though some of the insurance industry's enormous profits have decreased recently due largely to natural disaster losses, "private passenger vehicle coverage is now 'by far the largest line of insurance and is currently the most important source of industry profits.'"[13]

Nor have the carriers passed along to their customers any of the additional dollars they have earned by squeezing soft tissue injury victims. As Drew Griffin and Kathleen Johnson pointed out in their article entitled "Auto Insurers Play Hardball in Minor Crash Claims,"

The result [of the claims handling changes since the mid-1990s] has been billions in profits for insurance companies and little, if anything, for the public, according to University of Nevada insurance law professor Jeff Stempel.

"We can see that policyholders individually are getting hurt by being dragged through the court on fender-bender claims, and yet we don't see any collateral benefit in the form of reduced premiums even for the other policyholders," Stempel said.

"So I think now we can say to continue this kind of program is in my view institutionalized bad faith."[14]

---

12 *From Good Hands to Boxing Gloves*, by David Berardinelli, Trial Guides LLC (2006, 2008), p. 64.

13 "Private Auto Insurance is the Biggest Source of Industry Profits," *Online Auto Insurance News*, by Matthew Morisset (December 7, 2011), http://news. onlineautoinsurance.com/companies/private-car-insurance-profits-report-95713, citing a report from the Insurance Information Institute.

14 "Auto Insurers Play Hardball in Minor Crash Claims," by Drew Griffin and Kathleen Johnston, CNN.com (February 9, 2007); http://www.cnn.com/2007/ US/02/09/insurance.hardball/index.html.

3. The Power of Advertising (or Tell Us How Great You Are and We Shall Believe)

It's ironic that just as Allstate, State Farm, and other carriers began to treat accident victims unfairly, they embarked on numerous media campaigns telling us how wonderful they were. Allstate even spent money publishing misleading ads about the percentages of each premium dollar they were paying out in claims.[15] All of those millions saved on claims allowed these companies the increasing luxury of coming into our living rooms on a daily basis to deliver a continual televised brainwashing—and that's exactly what it is, brainwashing. I often meet with people who say things like "that adjuster was being so unfair, but I know they're a good company, so I just don't understand it." It usually turns out that the client's only reason for thinking the company was "good" was because the company's advertising had continually said as much. Considering that *GEICO alone spent nearly a billion dollars in advertising in 2011,* [16] this type of thinking is understandable. I also find it ironic that GEICO chose a gecko as its "spokesperson" considering that it was the infamous Gordon Gekko in the movie *Wallstreet* who uttered the words, "Greed, for lack of a better word, is good."

Well, insurance carriers are all very good at taking your premium money, there's absolutely no argument about that. And if you miss a payment, they're extremely good (and efficient) about cancelling your policy. There won't be any *delay* at all. But, once a wreck happens, you're stuck with that carrier and you may need representation.

4. Won't Your Own Company Help You After a Wreck?

What about your own insurance company? Certainly, they'll be there to fight for you after a wreck? WRONG. Unfortunately, too many people

---

15 *From Good Hands to Boxing Gloves*, by David Berardinelli, Trial Guides LLC (2006, 2008), pp. 37–8.

16 In 2011, GEICO spent $993.8 million in advertising, while State Farm spent $813.5 million and Progressive spent $536.1 million. "Allstate Profit Quadruples as Storm Claims Costs Decline," *Bloomberg*, by Noah Buhayar (October 31, 2012), http://www.bloomberg.com/news/print/2012-10-31/allstate-profit-quadruples-as-storm-claims-costs-decline.html.

believe the fiction that their carrier's job is to assist them after a wreck that was someone else's fault. As a result, they often don't realize the truth until it is too late.

Your own insurance company is not obligated to "represent" you, or your interests. Nowhere in your insurance policy (that most people have never read) does it say or require that your insurance company is obligated to help you. And, believe me, if it is not in your insurance policy, they are NOT going to do it.

Nor do insurance companies "fight for you" after you've been in a wreck. They are designed to fight for themselves and their own interests. If winning an argument with the other driver's insurance company means your company will not have to pay the other driver's damages, then your company might argue with the other carrier. If your company wins that argument, you may benefit. *But, they are not fighting for you; they are fighting for themselves and their money.*

Often, your company has nothing to gain by arguing with the other carrier. In that case, you are on your own. For instance, your company has no interest in fighting to make sure the other driver's carrier pays you fairly for your vehicle. And they certainly have no interest in fighting to make sure that the other driver's carrier pays you fairly for your injuries. In fact, many companies don't even explain to their customers how the customer's own policy can help them after a wreck. Or, the carrier will attempt to dissuade its customers from using valuable coverage the customer has paid for by telling the customer their "rates will go up." This type of "advice" is probably unethical, in violation of many state insurance codes, and often costs injured people thousands of dollars they can ill afford to lose at a critical time in their lives.[17]

Moreover, many folks who are in wrecks quickly find that their insurance agent (i.e., the person who sold them the policy) is not very helpful or knowledgeable regarding the insurance claim process. This is because insurance agents specialize in *selling insurance*. The people who specialize in *handling claims* are the insurance adjusters. Personally,

---

17 I find that carriers often tell this to the insured regarding the use of medical payments coverage. The use and importance of this coverage is discussed in Chapter VI, Part B of this book.

I believe that the agents and adjusters are separated so that the carriers can maintain a "good cop, bad cop" system. The good cop is the local guy you may know from the community who comes to your home and sells you the insurance. The "bad cop" is the adjuster who only comes around when there's a problem (i.e., a claim) and then tells you your car isn't worth as much as you thought, or your injury isn't really that bad. The carrier would prefer that you get mad at the adjuster rather than the agent. Hopefully, you'll think it's not the agent's fault and continue to buy insurance from him, even though his colleague just short-changed you.

So, just remember, your own insurance company does not represent you or your interests after a wreck—it's just not their job.

B. What Insurance Companies Do

After the other driver's insurance company has notice of a wreck, they generally begin to take action very quickly.

1. Investigate to See if You Are Partly to Blame

The first thing the other driver's company will do is investigate the wreck. This usually involves obtaining recorded statements from the drivers and possibly talking to the police. When the adjuster contacts you, however, he or she is not asking to take your statement just for kicks; they are taking the statement to see if there is any possibility he or she can claim that you were fully, or partially, to blame for the wreck.

In states like Indiana, where the law follows a principle called "comparative fault," assessing the innocent driver with some part of the blame can pay big dividends for insurance companies. For instance, if a company has 1,000 auto wreck claims a year and the average payment per claim is $7,500—that is a total payout of $7,500,000. If that company can assess 20% of the fault on those wrecks to the other driver, that's a savings of $1,500,000 a year (enough to pepper the local air waves with a whole new series of commercials telling us how wonderful the carrier is).

Even worse, Indiana has a different liability standard if you are in a wreck with a vehicle owned or operated by a city, county, or the state. In that case, the law follows a principle called "contributory fault." *Under this principle, if you are even 1% responsible for the wreck and the governmental entity is 99% responsible, you are not entitled to one penny of compensation!* So, adjusters in these types of cases have an even greater incentive to trip you up on a recorded statement.

It doesn't take much for some companies to try to assess fault against you. Once you've said something on tape, regardless of whether it's just an off-the-cuff remark, or even a joke, you're stuck with it.

2. <u>Sugar or Salt?</u>

Insurance adjusters may be nice to accident victims, or they may be rude. They may call constantly, or they may not call at all (and be impossible to reach). They may offer a quick settlement (for a very low amount), or they may string the case along. Adjuster actions are determined by 1) their strategy, 2) their case load, and 3) their personality.

The point is: even if they act sweet and helpful, it's not because they really care about you; it's because they really care about getting you to accept the lowest possible settlement offer.

Accident victims are often lulled into a false sense of security by adjusters who pretend to really care.[18] The adjuster might say she will "take care of everything." So, the injured person proceeds to obtain medical treatment and have the bills forwarded to the adjuster. The adjuster then proceeds to let the bills sit on his or her desk and collect dust. I have met with people who thought the other driver's carrier was paying their medical bills. This often goes on for several months until the injured person gets a collection notice in the mail. The adjuster then has this person right where they want them—desperate and dependent on their low-ball settlement offer to get out of debt. After

---

18   I do not mean to infer that insurance adjusters are all inhuman monsters with no feelings. Sometimes, their expressions of sympathy are real. Yet, even real sympathy will not override their job responsibility which is to get their employer out of the claim as cheaply as possible.

tne person hires me and I call the adjuster to find out why they told the client they were paying his or her bills, I often get a response like, "Well ...I told him I *wanted* to pay his bills, and I asked him to send them to me, but I never actually said I *would* pay them." Very slick.

When an injured person's vehicle damage claim is handled quickly and easily, this often gives them false hope that their injury claim will be handled fairly. The thought is: "If it was that easy to have my car repaired or totaled out, surely they will do the same when it comes time to resolve my injury claim." It's a reasonable theory and one that the insurance companies encourage and nurture. In fact, it's part of their strategy. Unfortunately, I have seen this theory proven wrong hundreds of times. *Easy resolution of a property damage claim does not mean easy resolution of the bodily injury claim, even when fault is clear.* In fact, as Jay Feinman stated

> If the property damage issues are handled quickly and to the claimant's satisfaction, it makes the claimant believe that the company is interested in a fair and favorable resolution, which means the company may be able to pay less on the larger personal injury damages.[19]

Sometimes, on the other hand, adjusters will act mean and tough and try to make you feel guilty about making a claim. This strategy also works. Many people simply give up and knuckle under to tough insurance adjusting tactics. They just figure it's not worth all the hassle. Others really do feel guilty about making a claim. They subconsciously associate themselves with the so-called "fakers" out there that the insurance companies want us to believe are so prevalent. People who are hurt in wrecks often feel like everyone, including the adjuster on the other side, will think they are one of the "fakers" even though they really are hurt. So, instead of standing up for their rights, these people feel guilty and would rather settle for something they know is not fair, just to avoid being thought of in an unfavorable light. Insurance companies love this! That's why they make such a big deal out of a faker when they catch one.

---

19 *Delay, Deny, Defend;* Jay M. Feinman, Portfolio (2010), p. 89.

Faking accidents and injuries is *very* infrequent. Yet, by publicizing a faker when one is caught, the insurance carriers feed the misconception that faking is rampant. Making the general public believe that faking is rampant 1) poisons juries against *everyone* who is injured in a wreck, 2) makes people who are legitimately injured feel guilty about making a claim, and 3) helps the carriers get politicians on their side so that restrictive laws can be enacted which make personal injury claims more difficult to win (even though there is no legitimate underlying basis for the law).

III.WHAT YOU SHOULD DO—AND NOT DO—WHEN YOU'VE BEEN IN A WRECK

A. Call the Police

When you've been in a wreck, regardless of who was at fault, make sure the police are called to the scene. Do not let the other driver talk you into exchanging information and driving off. First, in many jurisdictions (depending on the amount of the vehicle damage and whether there are injuries), contacting the police after a wreck is mandatory. There is no point in compounding the misery of being in a wreck by risking a charge of leaving the scene of an accident.

B. Leave Your Car Where it is—Unless Its Location is a Danger

If you move your vehicle immediately after a wreck, your actions may make it very difficult for the police and the insurance companies to determine whose fault the wreck was. On the other hand, if you are in a minor rear-end collision with no vehicle damage, leaving your car in a busy intersection or highway could present an unnecessary danger to you or the other drivers on the road.

C. Take Photographs

It's always a good idea to obtain photographs of the damage to the vehicles and even the accident scene and vehicle positions. The police rarely take photos at the scene of a wreck unless there are significant injuries or a fatality (if the police do take photographs at the scene of your wreck, you will not need to take any). In this day and age where everyone has a camera built into their cell phone, it should be easy for most folks to snap several photos while still at the scene, unless you are injured too badly. In that case, a photo will be the last thing on your mind. Also, if you cannot take photographs safely--do not risk further injury by attempting to take photos at the scene.

It's now well known that there is no correlation between the damage to a vehicle and the damage to the bodies inside the vehicle. *See* Chapter VIII, Part A of this book. Someone can have injuries that require surgery when their vehicle sustained only minor damage. Conversely, many people have walked away from wrecks with no injuries where the damage to the vehicles is tremendous. Yet, it's still nice to see exactly what the vehicles looked like following the wreck instead of relying on eyewitness testimony that could be given years later if the case ends up in court. Even if you did not take photographs at the scene, you can take them once your vehicle is home; or, if the vehicle is towed, you can take photos at the storage facility.

The insurance carriers will sometimes take their own photographs. Of course, they will seldom give these to you unless there is a lawsuit. We are finding that insurance adjusters are being more selective in the photographs they take. If there is no visible damage, or very little damage to your car, then you can be certain that they will take many photos from all angles. If, on the other hand, there is significant damage, they will not take photographs. The adjusters are no longer attempting to simply document the damage, or lack thereof. Instead, they are trying to take photographs that can be used against you at trial.

D. Do Not Give a Recorded Statement (with Certain Exceptions)

The insurance adjuster for the other driver involved in a wreck will almost always call you to discuss the wreck and ask if they can record your statement. As mentioned earlier, this can be very dangerous. Even though you will tell the truth and you have absolutely nothing to hide, giving a recorded statement is still dangerous. You may think, "It's a simple story, the wreck wasn't my fault," and you may be right. However, the adjuster is not really calling to "get your side of the story." Indeed, if that were all he or she wanted, they would not need to record the conversation. Instead, they could just review the police report and expedite the processing of your claim.

Once the preliminary "name, rank, and serial number" questions have been completed, the adjuster may ask questions about how quickly you came to a stop, when you started to slow down, whether your brake lights were working, your previous medical history, your previous accident history, whether you were hurt at the scene, etc. They may seem like they're your friend, and some of these questions might seem innocuous, but the questions have a purpose.

For instance, you might say that you were going to go through the intersection "but saw the yellow light and hit your brakes." A simple statement like that might be used against you later when the adjuster claims that you stopped short because you were not paying close attention to the road. You might say you were going "about 55 mph." Later, the adjuster might claim that you were not certain of your speed and therefore may well have been speeding. Perhaps you tell the adjuster that you "didn't really see the other driver" that ran the stop sign, until he or she pulled out in front of you. The adjuster may then claim that if you were being careful, you would have seen the other driver before then.

Similarly, the adjuster may contact you hours after the wreck and ask if you were hurt in the wreck. You may tell them no. However, there is often a delay in the onset of soft tissue injury pain. So, if you wake up the next day with severe neck pain and go to the doctor, the adjuster may claim that you told them you had no injuries and now you are making a false claim. If you really have neck pain, it must be due to something else. Maybe you just slept funny?

Insurance adjusters often try to take recorded statements of people who are on narcotic pain medication and even people who have been admitted to the hospital in serious condition. Adjusters sometimes even go to the injured person's hospital room. Luckily, once the insurance company receives a letter of representation from an attorney, all direct contacts with the injured person must cease.

The exception to refraining from giving a recorded statement may be in a situation where the carrier asking for the statement is *your own insurance company*. Depending on your policy language, you may have a duty to cooperate with your carrier. That duty could include giving them a statement. Whether the statement must be recorded or not could also depend on specific policy language. Also, remember that in certain situations (like uninsured and underinsured motorist claims) you may wind up in an adversarial position with your carrier; therefore, you should be careful about the scope of any statement you give them.

Consequently, if you are injured in a wreck and are contacted by any adjuster requesting a recorded statement, it may be a good idea to discuss the situation with a personal injury attorney.

E. <u>Go to the Hospital if You Have Pain or Do Not Feel Well</u>

We will discuss this at a later point in the book, but if you have pain after a wreck, or even if you do not feel "right," you are best served by going to the emergency room. I am not saying, however, that you should go to the hospital if you feel absolutely fine and are having zero problems.

Just remember that adrenaline is a funny thing. I have had hundreds (maybe thousands) of clients over the last 27 years who have not felt much pain after a wreck, but then began having pain once the initial rush or shock of the wreck began to wear off. In fact, this has happened to me.

I was driving on a southeastern Indiana highway with my wife, our friend, and my daughter one afternoon. We were on our way to my son's junior high football game, when a young woman crossed the centerline and was coming at us in our lane of travel. She was trying to pass a semi on a double yellow line. I swerved out of her way, but we still collided. After the impact, my SUV remained on the highway while her car ran off into the woods. I quickly checked on all of my passengers and then jumped out and ran into the woods to see if the other driver was OK. Once I determined that she did not have life-threatening injuries, I trotted back up the hill to my SUV to assess the damage. I felt no pain at all, not even slight soreness. It wasn't until I reached for my registration about 30 minutes after the wreck that I felt a "funny" feeling in my side. It just tingled, but didn't really hurt. After an hour or two, it finally began to hurt and, as it turned out, I had three broken ribs from the shoulder harness grabbing and stopping my forward progress. Yet I had no marks or bruises on my chest.

I also recently had a trial where my client had a similar delayed reaction to an injury after a wreck. The first witness we put on the stand was the investigating police officer. He testified that over the years he had investigated hundreds of wrecks. During that time, he had been involved in numerous situations where people initially seemed to be pain free and uninjured. He often arrived at the scene to find them walking around talking (just happy to still be alive). Sometimes, however, as time went on, he might see that same person eventually lie down next to the road in agony, literally unable to move; or, he sometimes found out that someone who did not appear to be injured at the scene, was later diagnosed with a serious injury in the emergency room.

Sometimes people who know they are hurt at the scene of a wreck still refuse to go to the hospital because they don't want to incur the cost of treatment. Over the next several weeks, the pain and soreness increases, but they still hold off on treatment—until finally they can no longer stand it. By waiting two, three, or four weeks to seek medical attention, these people have not only caused themselves additional pain and stress, but they have also played right into the insurance company's hands. The insurance company will now attempt to use several arguments against these folks: 1) How bad could it have been if the guy didn't even seek treatment? 2) It's not our fault he's not better now. If he had just gotten immediate medical attention, he would not be in this condition; and 3) How do we know it was the wreck that hurt his back? It's been 30 days since the wreck and he might have done something else during that time to hurt his back.

F. If You Are Injured, Call a Good and Experienced Personal Injury Attorney Right Away!

If you are injured in a wreck, you should call an experienced personal injury attorney. *People who hire good attorneys wind up being compensated with more money than people who attempt to handle claims on their own.* If you don't believe me, let's look at some figures that came from the insurance industry.

One study of uninsured motorist claims concluded that represented policyholders recovered 90 percent more than those without lawyers ...In general, represented claimants recovered two to five times as much as those without the aid of a lawyer.[1]

This is why insurance carriers try so hard to discourage people from hiring attorneys. It's why McKinsey, from the beginning of its engagement with Allstate, made one of its major objectives to "keep attorney out."[2]

I am not saying, however, that just contacting any old lawyer is necessarily a great idea. In today's world, the guy who prepared your will or handled your home closing may not be the best guy to handle your personal injury case. There are many firms in every state that concentrate on personal injury law. That's where I'd go. If I need surgery on my hand, I'm going to a hand surgeon, not my family doctor or someone who does vasectomies.

G. Reasons Often Given for Not Hiring an Attorney

The most common reasons given for why people don't call an attorney right away after they've been injured in a wreck are: 1) "I didn't think I was hurt too badly;" 2) "I didn't want to sue that person, they just made a mistake;" 3) "I didn't want to pay someone to do something I should be able to do myself;" and 4) "The insurance adjuster said if I got a lawyer, it would take years and the lawyer would end up with all the money."

Let's address these one at a time:

1. "I didn't think I was hurt too badly"

When you have no large lacerations or broken bones, but rather have what appears to be a soft tissue injury, it's often difficult to tell just how badly you're injured. Many people don't ever go to a health care provider because they say they "expect to be sore." It's not until they either don't get better, or get worse, that they seek medical treatment.

---

1 *Delay, Deny, Defend;* Jay M. Feinman, Portfolio (2010), p. 88.
2 *Delay, Deny, Defend;* Jay M. Feinman, Portfolio (2010), p. 89.

Some people are in extreme pain several days after a wreck, yet go on to make a full recovery in 30–60 days. Other people who initially just had some neck soreness sometimes wind up needing cervical fusion surgery. The point is, with these kinds of injuries, it may not always be easy to determine the extent of the injury until months after the wreck.

Regardless of how long the injury lasts, you are still better off consulting a good and experienced personal injury attorney. If the claim is too small, a good lawyer will tell the potential clients not to hire them. They will give them advice on what to do and send them on their way without charging them a penny.

If, however, an attorney believes they can help someone have their bills paid and receive better (and more fair) compensation than they can obtain themselves, they will take the case and help them— even if they don't make a "profit." Why would a law firm do this? Because a good attorney cares about people. Every time an insurance company is prevented from steamrolling someone, everyone out there who has, or may have, a claim is helped. It's also good business practice to send a happy customer out into the community. We are in the business of fighting insurance companies when they are treating people unfairly. The size of the case shouldn't matter. The principle is the same.

2. "I didn't want to sue that person, they just made a mistake"

Some people do not want to sue anyone. The truth is, virtually every personal injury attorney resolves more cases before suit is filed than after suit is filed. A lawsuit is often only filed when an insurance company is being completely unreasonable.

Unfortunately, without the leverage of having an attorney standing behind you who *will* file a lawsuit if necessary, you are left with little or no bargaining power. When you are up against a billion-dollar insurance company, having no bargaining power puts you at a distinct, and often fatal, disadvantage.

3. "I didn't want to pay someone to do something I should be able to do myself"

Just because you *should* be able to handle your own claim in a perfect world does not mean that you *can* handle your own claim effectively in this less-than-perfect world. Just because you might be able to build a seven-foot stone wall in your backyard doesn't mean that you can do it as well as an experienced stone mason.

There are a huge number of complications people run into when they have been injured in a wreck due to all of the different insurance coverage provisions involved. Successfully navigating this maze of coverages is extremely difficult for the average person. We even see lawyers who do not regularly handle injury cases make multiple mistakes on claims. There are certain laws and insurance provisions that must be complied with in order to make a recovery. Not knowing these laws and provisions can negatively impact a case.

Complications in injury cases are often compounded when hospitals and doctors' offices give injured people poor advice on how bills should be paid. With private health insurance, Medicare, Medicaid, short-term disability, and your own auto insurance potentially being involved—seeking the help of a professional is the safest option.

4. "The insurance adjuster said if I got a lawyer, it would take years and the lawyer would end up with all the money."

Although insurance adjusters often tell people this to dissuade them from hiring an attorney, nothing could be further from the truth. A lawyer has no incentive to allow a case to drag on for years. Think about it—injury attorneys take cases on a contingency fee agreement—they get nothing unless and until the case is resolved. So, if there is a case where the client is scheduled to finish their medical treatment on October 1, when October 1 rolls around, a good personal injury lawyer will request all of the client's medical records and bills and have a package ready to go out to the insurance carrier as soon as those records and bills come into their office.

In fact, injured people with good and experienced personal injury attorneys can almost always settle their cases <u>faster</u> than people attempting to handle claims on their own. The reason is simple—if you try to settle the case on your own, you put the adjuster in control and he or she is in no hurry. When an experienced lawyer handles a case, they are in control and they are pushing as hard and as fast as they can.

If you represent yourself, the adjuster will require you to give them a medical release and he or she will obtain your medical bills and records on their own. Once the adjuster has finally gotten everything (assuming they ever do), they then *might* try to settle the case with you. However, they're in no hurry because the longer the insurance company keeps your money, the longer they can keep it invested and make money (remember the "float"). Additionally, you may never know which records and bills the adjuster has and which they do not. If he or she tells you they never received Dr. Smith's last bill, or that they "misplaced" it and will need to ask for it again, you don't know whether they're telling the truth or not. Also, the medical release the adjuster makes you sign may allow them to talk to the doctors behind your back and request any kind of medical record he or she wants, no matter how irrelevant or private. *When you have an attorney, they get the medical records and bills.* They index them and bind them and give them to the insurance company and let the company know that the lawyer has provided the company with everything they need to evaluate the case. They then ask for a reasonable response date and follow-up until they receive a response. The lawyer never lets the insurance adjuster talk to your doctors. The adjusters should not be permitted to tell your doctors how to treat you.

Anyone who has ever attempted to resolve an injury claim on their own will tell you that one of the greatest challenges you face is actually getting the adjuster on the phone. It's funny how often the adjuster calls, and how accessible he or she is, when they want something from you. But it's sad how inaccessible he or she often is when you need them. There are a number of different techniques we have developed over the years to deal with this problem. Suffice it to say, they can run for a little while, but they can't hide from us for too long (without repercussions)!

The argument that the lawyer will "take all the money" is equally false. A case cannot be settled unless the client gives the lawyer permission to do so. Before requesting permission, the lawyer goes through the numbers and the client knows exactly what they will end up with. I don't believe that I have ever had a case in 27 years where we got paid and the client got nothing. Why would a client do that? Why would I do that? Our goal is to send former customers out into the world equipped to recommend, not condemn, our firm. Lawyers who don't get referrals or recommendations from former clients, probably aren't very good lawyers.

H. <u>Additional Reasons to Hire a Good and Experienced Personal Injury Attorney</u>

A good and experienced personal injury attorney will have investigators who can talk to witnesses and do accident reconstruction immediately following the wreck. A good and experienced personal injury attorney will help you resolve your vehicle damage claim (we do this free of charge), coordinate payment of your medical bills, and tell you whether you should use health insurance and/or your personal auto medical payments coverage. A good and experienced personal injury attorney will also coordinate payment of all of your bills and make sure that you fulfill all of the contractual provisions in your health insurance and auto insurance contracts. These contracts may mandate that your carrier is notified of the wreck and properly repaid at the end of the case. Your lawyer will take care of this. A good and experienced personal injury attorney will even fight for discounts on those repayments that you may not be eligible to obtain on your own.

Finally, a good and experienced personal injury attorney will know what your case is worth. Knowing what a case is worth is like a real estate agent knowing the approximate value of a house. If you wanted to sell your house, but you had no idea what any of the other houses in the neighborhood had ever sold for, how would you know how to price your house? You wouldn't. You might price your house too low, thinking it's just three bedrooms and only two bathrooms. You might not have realized things a good realtor would know about your house, such as: 1) it's the smallest house in a neighborhood of larger, more expensive homes;

2) it's on a quiet cul-de-sac; 3) it's in the most desirable school system in the city, etc. On the other hand, you might price your house too high and never be able to sell it if you were too emotionally attached to the house because of all the work you did on it and because it was where you raised your children. To a prospective purchaser, though, your home is simply a nice three-bedroom, two-bath home. Your emotional attachment to the home does not make it worth twice as much as the other three-bedroom, two-bath houses the potential purchasers have visited.

IV. WHAT IS A SOFT TISSUE INJURY?

A. Our Definition of "Soft Tissue Injury"

Most people don't say they have a "soft tissue injury" when they're injured in a car wreck or in some other occurrence. They may say they have "whiplash" or "a neck injury" or a "back sprain." However, doctors, chiropractors, lawyers, and insurance adjusters often refer to these injuries as "soft tissue." So, if you've been injured in a wreck and don't have any broken bones, chances are that somewhere along the line someone will use the term "soft tissue injury" to describe your problem. Therefore, it's a good idea to know what that term means.

In this book, when talking about "soft tissue" injuries, we are referring to injuries to muscles, tendons, and ligaments. This is the generally accepted definition of a "soft tissue injury."

Primarily, we will be talking about neck and back injuries where there are no fractures, bone chips, or herniated discs. Instead, what are commonly called "soft tissue injuries," are injuries to the connective tissues of the spine. Connective tissues "bind, support, and protect the human body and its vital organs."[1]

"The role of *ligaments*, which connect bone to bone, are to augment the mechanical stability of joints, to guide motion, and to prevent excessive motion. The function of *tendons* is to attach muscle to bone and transmit tensile loads, thereby producing joint motion."[2] Tendons and ligaments are relatively "tough," fibrous entities, but they are still categorized as "soft" tissue since they are generally much "softer" than bone or cartilage.

While ligaments and tendons cannot be seen on X-ray and MRI, there are occasions when a doctor can view an X-ray or an MRI and give an opinion that there has been stretching and/or tearing of these tissues due to abnormal spacing the doctor sees between the bone. In

---

1 *Accidental Injury: Biomechanics and Prevention*, Springer-Verlag (1993), Chapter 10, "Biomechanics of Soft Tissues," by Roger Haut, p. 224.

2 Id., p. 230.

fact, motion X-rays are designed to diagnose this very condition in the spine.[3]

Often, you will see soft tissue injuries referred to as "sprains" or "strains." The two terms do not necessarily have clear and consistent definitions. Sometimes, medical providers will use both terms and simply state that their patient had a "sprain/strain." Sometimes, however, a doctor will state in a report, or a medical record, that the client had a "sprain." Sometimes, an injury is simply referred to as a "strain." There would be no confusion if everyone's definition of these terms were the same. Unfortunately, that's not the case.

According to *Stedman's Medical Dictionary (27th Ed.)*, a sprain is "an injury to a ligament as a result of abnormal or excessive forces applied to a joint, but without dislocation or fracture." A strain, on the other hand, is defined in the same dictionary as "to injure by use or overuse."

Physicians and chiropractors, however, many times use the term "strain" to refer to stretching or tearing of muscles or tendons, and "sprain" to refer to stretching or tearing of ligaments. This definition seems to be approved by the Mayo Clinic. In fact, according to Mayo-clinic.com,

> Sprains and strains are common injuries that share similar signs and symptoms. A sprain is a stretching or tearing of ligaments—the tough bands of fibrous tissue that connect one bone to another in your joints... A strain is a stretching or tearing of muscles or tendon. A tendon is a fibrous cord of tissue that connects muscles to bones...[4]

Similarly, the American Academy of Orthopedic Surgeons states that

> [t]he joints of your body are supported by ligaments. Ligaments are strong bands of connective tissue that connect one bone to another. A sprain is a simple stretch or tear of the ligaments... Your bones are supported by a combination of

---

3 See http://www.dmxworks.com/ for a full description of motion X-rays.

4 www.mayoclinic.com/health/sprains-and-strains/DS00343.

muscles and tendons. Tendons connect muscles to bones. A strain is the result of an injury to either a muscle or a tendon, usually in your foot or leg. The strain may be a simple stretch in your muscle or tendon, or it may be a partial or complete tear in the muscle-and-tendon combination.[5]

However, in a well-respected book on soft tissue injuries, a "sprain" is described as "a traumatic over-stretching or tearing of ligaments or tendons encompassing a joint. A "strain" is defined as "an injury to the muscle or ligamentous structures."[6]

As a result of the confusion caused by the various definitions described above, it's important to find out exactly what a doctor means when the doctor describes a soft tissue injury as a "sprain," "strain," or "sprain/strain." In any event, one thing is certain—sprains and strains are considered soft tissue injuries.

B. The Mechanism of a Soft Tissue Injury

The classic "whiplash" scenario occurs in an auto wreck when someone is hit from behind. This type of collision often produces a soft tissue injury to the cervical spine (i.e., the neck area). In fact, "[w]hiplash injuries are the most frequent cause of cervical sprains and strains, with over 1 million cases in the United States every year."[7] Consequently, "the biomechanics of the 'whiplash' injury mechanism have been studied more extensively than any other injury."[8] In fact, there is a wealth of data available on the subject.

In addition to being called "whiplash," what often happens to your body in a rear-end collision is also often referred to as an injury caused by "flexion-extension" and/or "acceleration/deceleration." As your vehicle

---

5   http://orthoinfo.aaos.org/topic.cfm?topic=A00304

6   *Soft Tissue Injuries: Diagnosis and Treatment,* Hanley & Belfus, inc. (1998) Edited by Windsor and Lox, "Cervical Soft Tissue Injuries," by F. Falco, MD, F. Lagattuta, MD, et.al., p.21.

7   *Soft Tissue Injuries Diagnosis and Treatment,* Hanley & Belfus, by Robert E. Windsor and Dennis M. Lox, MD (1998), p. 21.

8   Id.

is struck from behind, your vehicle accelerates forward. When the vehicle accelerates, so do you—or at least your torso and shoulders—while your neck and head lag behind in what is called "hyperextension."[9] This is followed by rapid forward flexion and then extension again.[10]

The peak acceleration of the head in even a five mph rear-end collision is "considerably greater than that of the car" and is "followed by significant deceleration."[11] This means that when you are hit from behind and your car lurches forward, your head snaps backward faster than your car moves forward. Then, that fast snapping stops suddenly (i.e., this is the "deceleration"). This sudden stopping puts a great deal of stress on the human body. It's not the motion that necessarily causes injury, but rather the quick stopping and the time involved. Or, as a doctor once told me when we were preparing for a trial, "It's not the fall from the building that hurts you—it's the sudden stop when you hit the ground!"

After snapping backward, the head then rebounds forward (bouncing off the seat). The backward motion happens so fast that most people in rear end collisions only recall the forward motion. They will often say that when they were hit, their head "went forward toward the steering wheel," without realizing that, immediately prior, their head snapped backwards.

Wearing a seatbelt can save your life by keeping you from being thrown from a vehicle. *However, being strapped to the seat of your car with our ever-improving safety belts and harnesses can actually make a soft tissue injury worse.*[12] This is due to the fact that the torso remains more fixed, or strapped in, while the head and neck still move back-

---

9   *Soft Tissue Injuries Diagnosis and Treatment*, Hanley & Belfus, by Robert E. Windsor and Dennis M. Lox, MD (1998), p. 21; *Humane Medicine Healthcare*, Volume 7 Number 3 (2007), by Robert Teasell, MD FRCPC, Glenn R. McCain, MD FRCPC, Harold Mersky, DM FRCPC, Hillel Finestone, MD CCFP FRCPC http://www.humanehealthcare.com/Article.asp?art_id=330.

10   Id.

11   *Soft Tissue Injuries Diagnosis and Treatment*, Hanley & Belfus, by Robert E. Windsor and Dennis M. Lox, MD (1998), p. 22.

12   *Humane Medicine Healthcare*, Volume 7 Number 3 (2007), by Robert Teasell, MD FRCPC, Glenn R. McCain, MD FRCPC, Harold Mersky, DM FRCPC, Hillel Finestone, MD CCFP FRCPC.

ward, forward, and compress, thereby accentuating the "whipping" action of the trauma.

Learning more about the true mechanism of an injury helps everyone involved understand how someone could still have neck pain months after a car wreck. In a courtroom, it's always more effective to fully describe this process (preferably with diagrams and models) than it is to simply say, "Mary was hit from behind by a pick-up truck and got whiplash." Having a well-spoken chiropractor or physician describe the mechanism of a flexion-extension injury while using simple visual aids can go a long way toward allowing a jury to understand what actually happens to a client's body at the moment of impact. With appropriate visualization, it's much easier to see how neck muscles, tendons, and ligaments could become stretched or torn in a rear-end collision.

A clear understanding, description, and visualization of the mechanism of injury are even more important in a soft tissue case than many other injury cases. Without lacerations, X-rays showing fractures, or MRIs showing herniations or tears, the average soft tissue injury case starts off at a distinct disadvantage. This disadvantage is often compounded when lawyers fail to discuss the true mechanism of the injury.[13]

---

13 See *David Ball on Damages 3*, by David Ball, PhD NITA (2011), p. 150.

V. SOFT TISSUE INJURY SYMPTOMS AFTER A WRECK

Sometimes clients who sustain soft tissue injuries in car wrecks will report pain at the accident scene to the investigating police officers. If clients complain of pain at the scene, this will usually be noted in the police report. The officer can testify regarding what he was told by the client immediately following the wreck. In minor property damage wrecks, this can be especially helpful testimony.

A. Can There Be A Delay Before You Feel Pain?

It is entirely possible for someone to suffer a soft tissue injury without reporting pain at the wreck site, being treated by paramedics, or going to the emergency room. In fact, even if they did not report back or neck pain in the emergency room, they may still have suffered a soft tissue injury. It is now well documented that there can be "a delay of up to three days" [1] (or longer) after the wreck before symptoms from a whiplash-type injury begin to occur. There is a more in-depth discussion of this issue in Chapter VIII, Part B of this book.

Despite the fact that delayed pain occurs frequently in soft tissue injury cases, insurance companies (and defense lawyers) will still claim that a delay in symptoms after a wreck means there could not have been an injury. This false assertion can be countered by the injured person's doctors citing their experience and the research. An analogy that is consistent with common experience is to compare post-wreck soreness with the soreness one gets after weight lifting, sprinting, or doing any relatively strenuous physical activity that you have not done for a while (or have never done). The soreness does not come imme-

---

1   National Institute of Neurological Disorders and Stroke, National Institutes of Health, Whiplash Information Page http://www.ninds.nih.gov/disorders/whiplash/whiplash.htm; *Humane Medicine Healthcare*, Volume 7 Number 3 (2007), by Robert Teasell, MD FRCPC, Glenn R. McCain, MD FRCPC, Harold Mersky, DM FRCPC, Hillel Finestone, MD CCFP FRCPC. P.2 http://www.humanehealthcare.com/Article.asp?art_id=330; *Whiplash Injuries: The Cervical Acceleration / Deceleration Syndrome*, Lippencott, Williams & Wilkins, by Stephen M. Foreman and Arthur C. Croft (2002), p. 359 ("It is not uncommon for pain to appear several days, and occasionally weeks, after the injury.")

diately after the activity. Rather, it is felt the following day or the day after that. Weight lifting, for example, involves stretching and tearing of muscles and soft tissues during the actual activity. Then, those tissues knit back together stronger than before to build muscle. The mechanism of injury in a wreck involves similar stretching and tearing with an often similar delay in pain. The difference between the two "activities," though, is that weight lifting is a controlled activity where joints are not "hyper" extended beyond their natural abilities or moved faster than they are designed to move.

While a delay in symptoms is a frequent occurrence in soft tissue injuries, as stated earlier, it is still critical for anyone who has been injured in a wreck to make sure they report all symptoms to their doctors and therapists as soon as they experience the symptoms. While individuals have little or no control over what their doctors actually write in the medical records, we tell clients that there is one certainty—*if you don't tell them about a symptom, it will never appear in the records*. Don't exaggerate your symptoms, but don't minimize them either.

B. <u>Symptom Documentation</u>

There are actually two issues to consider here: 1) soft tissue injuries may not cause any pain, or much pain, until several days (or longer) following the wreck or incident; and 2) even later than that, the client may be experiencing symptoms, but those symptoms may not appear in the medical records. There is nothing that can be done, pro-actively, about issue number one. However, issue number two can be avoided if an injured person receives good advice shortly after the wreck.

As we discussed earlier, people who are injured in wrecks should not postpone seeing a medical professional. Many people don't want to go to the doctor because they keep thinking, "It will get better." Before they know it, a month had passed. Unfortunately, waiting three or four weeks after a wreck to seek medical attention, or waiting three or four weeks after an initial emergency room visit to follow-up with a medical professional, plays right into the insurance company's hands. They argue that you must not have been hurt if you didn't seek treatment; or, they will say, "If you were hurt, your delay has made your recovery unnecessarily complicated." In either case, they will use it as an excuse to minimize your claim.

To avoid unwanted complications, *it's critical that anyone who is injured in a wreck seek immediate medical attention and report all symptoms, no matter how small, to all of their medical providers at every appointment.* Even so, we are often left with situations where a client begins with one set of complaints that appear to "morph" into a separate set of complaints three, four, or five weeks later. In fact, it can be the later-appearing complaints or symptoms that wind up being the more serious or permanent injuries.

For example, we recently tried a case for a very hard-working man who was a construction worker and a farmer. His case is very representative of the situation described above. His pickup truck was hit in the side and knocked off the road by a driver who crossed the centerline. The property damage was fairly impressive, but he did not feel much pain at the scene. He was taken by ambulance to the hospital where the emergency room physicians noted that he had "no real injury." His wife took him home and over the next few days he became progressively more sore and stiff. He aggravated a pre-existing back condition. This condition received most of the early attention from his family doctor and physical therapist. It wasn't until three weeks after the wreck that it was noted (by the therapist) that he had right knee pain. It turned out that the right knee was the most serious injury in the case.

Our client ultimately had an MRI months after the wreck. The MRI showed a torn meniscus, and the knee was eventually surgically repaired. But, the case went all the way to trial because right knee pain did not appear in the medical records until three weeks after the wreck. It wasn't his fault; he just wasn't a complainer. He hobbled around with pain all over his body, and it wasn't until much of that pain began to subside that he noticed the pain in his knee was still there. This is not unusual. In the end, it made no difference to the jury that the complaint took three weeks to appear in the records. The client's explanation for the delay in reporting made sense to the jury and was similar to experiences they had undergone in their own lives.

This type of delay in notation of symptoms happens all the time. If it can be avoided, that's great. If not, then it is critical to determine the reason(s) for the delay and figure out how to prove what happened. In the trial discussed above, our client was very honest and straightforward. His testimony, along with testimony from a couple of his friends and his wife, was very helpful. They said that he had been hurting all over and was limping around for the first couple of weeks after the wreck. His doctors also testified that his radiating back pain and other pain could have masked his knee pain to some extent.

There are other occasions when it's difficult for even trained physicians to determine the injury that is causing a certain set of symptoms. For instance, pain that is traveling from the top of the shoulder into the biceps and arm can be radiating pain originating from the client's neck due to a disc problem and pinched nerve, or it could be a shoulder injury—or both. Headaches can be due to a neck injury or a closed head post-concussion injury—or both. There are differences between the symptoms for these conditions, but it's up to the injured person to get to their doctor and do a good job answering questions and giving accurate descriptions so that their doctor can document, diagnose, treat, and ultimately (hopefully) cure the problem.

C. Pre-Existing Arthritis

It is very common in a personal injury case for someone to injure their neck or back in a wreck, have X-rays taken that day or shortly thereafter, and find out that the injured area has some form of pre-existing arthritis or spinal degeneration. Arthritis often shows up in X-rays taken of people in their 30s and 40s. It becomes more and more common as we enter our 50s and 60s. Virtually any arthritis or spinal degeneration that appears on X-ray immediately following a wreck was there before the wreck. This is because the arthritic process occurs over years, not days or months.

Many people are stunned by the fact that their X-rays showed pre-existing arthritis. They were stunned because they had no previous pain in that area. Often, however, the trauma of a car wreck triggers pain in the arthritic area. When pain is triggered in an arthritic area, it can be very difficult to make that pain to go away.

Sometimes, clients are not surprised by a post-wreck diagnosis of arthritis. They already knew they had arthritis because they had some previous pain and had undergone X-rays or an MRI before the wreck. These folks are even more vulnerable to the insurance adjuster's argument that "nothing came from the wreck because it was already there."

Insurance adjusters often act as if the discovery of pre-existing arthritis is a great thing for them; generally, they are wrong. Insurance adjusters will say, "Well they did an X-ray right after the wreck and he had arthritis in his back—that wasn't caused by the wreck." This is correct because, as stated above, arthritis takes years to occur. When, however, the insurance adjuster goes on to claim that "The pain Mr. Smith had after the wreck was just from the arthritis," they are wrong (unless he was having exactly the same pain the day before the wreck).

People with pre-existing arthritis are easier to hurt and harder to fix. Most doctors agree with this analysis. It seems that soft tissue injuries often aggravate pre-existing arthritis and make recovery much more difficult. Sometimes this occurs in people who have had prior pain and treatment and sometimes this occurs in people who had no previous pain or treatment. In this situation, the client's old medical records, going back several years before the wreck, must be requested. It's important to know exactly what types of problems the client was having before the wreck.

Sometimes a client's records showed previous complaints, even though the client said they had none. This is not because the client was being untruthful. Rather, they simply forgot. Complaining to a family doctor about lower back pain once or twice over three to five years is generally not a memorable event for most people—especially if the complaint was made during a visit for some other problem or ailment. The insurance carrier, though, will try to make these complaints into BIG events. When they see prior complaints and arthritis, the case can become very difficult to resolve. Often, it's necessary to file a lawsuit. Obviously, this can't be done without the assistance of an attorney.

However, an experienced personal injury attorney can turn the tables on the insurance carrier. An experienced lawyer can show that pre-existing arthritis actually helps to explain why clients can continue to have post-wreck pain and problems much longer than they otherwise might have had if, before the wreck, their spine had been completely healthy.

D. More Severe Symptoms and Injuries without "Direct Impact" to the Body

Anyone involved in a wreck who believes they have sustained a soft tissue injury with no cuts, broken bones, or direct impact to the head, should also be aware of other symptoms that could occur. There are three types of head injuries that accident victims can suffer without actually hitting their head inside the vehicle: 1) minor closed-head brain injuries; 2) injuries to the temporomandibular joint (TMJ) in the jaw, and 3) injuries to the soft tissue supporting structures of the jaw. While it is certainly possible to have these same injuries after hitting one's head, we are concerned here only with the possibility of an injury without direct contact.

1. Closed Head Injuries

Even though you may not hit your head on a hard surface inside your vehicle during a wreck, it's possible to injure your brain through a coup-contrecoup type mechanism. According to the CEMM[2] traumatic brain injury website, coup-contrecoup is described as follows:

---

2 "The CEMM is a dynamic initiative from the Office of the Air Force Surgeon General aimed at supplying the most powerful interactive technologies available to Medical Treatment Facilities (MTF), Health and Wellness Centers (HAWC), and TRICARE civilian medical facilities. The CEMM is a nationally recognized leader in patient-related interactive multimedia. Its innovative structure and sophisticated production outsourcing strategies position it perfectly for rapid response to the ever-changing needs of patients. To learn more, please visit their Web site at www.cemm. org; http://www.traumaticbraininjuryatoz.org/About-the-CEMM.aspx.

Coup-Contrecoup

A common way that a person can experience a traumatic brain injury is when an impact or violent motion brings their head to a sudden stop, causing the brain to slam into the skull. This is called a coup-contrecoup injury, also known as an acceleration/deceleration injury.

In this kind of injury, the brain bounces back and forth inside of the head, causing damage to the brain where it hits the skull. The brain is injured at the point of direct impact, and because it bounces back into the opposite side of the skull, the opposite side of the brain is injured as well.

Coup-contrecoup injuries can involve damage to the brain at the specific point of impact, called focal injuries, or to a large part of the brain, known as diffuse injuries.

It's important to know that coup-contrecoup injuries can happen as the result of trauma without direct impact to the head, since it is the movement of the brain inside of the skull that causes the injury.[3]

Additionally, there is research indicating that some whiplash sufferers, who don't even suffer a coup-contracoup injury, appear to suffer mild brain injuries in addition to other "normal" whiplash symptoms

The major symptoms reported after whiplash injuries are neck pain, upper back pain, headache, and muscle spasms. A subgroup of whiplash victims develop a chronic debility with somatic complaints, affective alterations, and depressed cognitive performance with particular problems in concentration and memory.[4]

* * *

---

3   http://www.traumaticbraininjuryatoz.org/mild-tbi/coup-contrecoup.aspx, emphasis added.

4   "Cerebral Symptoms After Whiplash Injury of the Neck: A Prospective Clinical and Neuropsychological Study of Whiplash Injury," *Journal of Neurology, Neurosurgery and Psychiatry*, by E. Ettlin, U. Kischka, S. Reichmann, et al. (1992) 55: at 943.

Electrophysiological studies also suggest that the functional abnormalities following whiplash injury evolve from disturbances in the midbrain, reticular formation, vestibular nuclei, and the hypothalamus, as well as the basal orbital and septal frontal regions. These areas are particularly prone to traumatic brain injury. [5]

2. Temporomandibular Joint Dysfunction

According to the National Institutes of Health,

The temporomandibular joint (TMJ) connects your jaw to the side of your head. When it works well, it enables you to talk, chew, and yawn. For people with TMJ dysfunction, problems with the joint and muscles around it may cause:

- Pain that travels through the face, jaw, or neck
- Stiff jaw muscles
- Limited movement or locking of the jaw
- Painful clicking or popping in the jaw
- A change in the way the upper and lower teeth fit together

Jaw pain may go away with little or no treatment. Treatment may include simple things you can do yourself, such as eating soft foods or applying ice packs. It may also include pain medicines or devices to insert in your mouth. In rare cases, you might need surgery.[6]

The TMJ can be injured in car wrecks through direct or indirect trauma.[7] In a TMJ injury without "direct" trauma, there is often a delay in the onset of the accident victim's overt symptoms.[8] Symptoms include

---

5   Id. at 947, citing "Psychiatric Aspects of Neurologic Disease," by M. Alexander, *Traumatic Brain Injury, Vol. 2,* New York: Grune and Stratton (1982) 219–48.

6   http://www.nlm.nih.gov/medlineplus/temporomandibularjointdysfunction.html.

7   *Soft Tissue Injuries: Diagnosis and Treatment,* Hanley & Belfus, inc. (1998) Edited by Windsor and Lox, "Temporomandibular Joint Dysfunction," by Chris Brown, DDS, MPS, pp. 230, 233.

8   Id. at 236.

audible popping and clicking of the jaw joint, jaw pain, inability to open the mouth uniformly (a feeling that the bite is "off"), ringing in the ear, etc.[9]

Sometimes people have the symptoms discussed above but don't associate the symptoms with their car wreck. It's critical for these people to get in to see someone who specializes in TMJ injuries as soon as possible. Some people with TMJ injuries delay treatment until they can no longer open their mouths completely. Obviously, "fixing" the problem is much more difficult once the TMJ deteriorates to this point.

3. Injuries to the Soft Tissue Supporting Structures of the Jaw

The lower jaw and upper jaw are connected by several ligaments. The lower jaw also has several ligaments that help support it but do not connect to the skull or upper jaw per se. These soft tissues can be injured without direct trauma. The injury can produce TMJ-like symptoms without any real damage to the jaw joints. A physical exam, and even an MRI, of the jaw may be negative, yet the patient can still feel pain and be unable to chew or open their mouth comfortably. These injuries may take weeks or even months to develop if there is no direct trauma. [10]

---

9   Id. at 228-9.

10   Information obtained from Chris Brown, DDS, MPS in direct consultation. Dental Diagnostic Services Hwy. 421 South, P.O. Box 685, Versailles, Indiana 47042

VI. HOW DO YOU PAY FOR MEDICAL TREATMENT AFTER A WRECK?

Before we talk about actual treatment options, it's important to talk about how the treatment will be paid for.

A. If You Have Health Insurance Should You Use it After a Wreck?

The answer to this question is "yes." Many people who have been injured in a wreck labor under the mistaken belief that they should not use their health insurance to pay their medical bills. This generally results in unpaid bills, adverse effects on credit ratings, and a weakening of the person's leverage with the insurance carrier. The loss of leverage is due to the fact that pressure to pay unpaid bills often leads to quick and desperate settlements.

Many times, people who are injured in wrecks don't use health insurance because they have been given bad instructions or advice. *Sometimes the doctor's offices and hospitals tell patients that they cannot use their health insurance after a wreck. This is incorrect.*

There is nothing in health insurance contracts that prohibits the use of the policy after a wreck. In fact, most policies state that health insurance *can* be used, but if the injured person receives a settlement, the health carrier must be repaid for the bills they paid out due to the wreck.

I have even seen hospitals that have contracts with a health insurer refuse to bill that insurer after a wreck. This may be a direct violation of the hospital's contract with the carrier. But, it doesn't stop them from misleading patients. In those instances, the health insurance company can be asked to call the provider and tell them they are in violation of the contract. The health insurance carriers are generally happy to help in this situation.

Medicare and Medicaid can be used just like any other form of health insurance and must also be repaid out of any settlement. However, while any provider who accepts Medicaid generally cannot refuse to accept your Medicaid, Medicare is a different story. Providers have the option of turning down or otherwise refusing to bill Medicare. That's why I advise clients who are having an expensive medical procedure performed as the result of a wreck to find out in advance from their provider (doctor, hospital, etc.) whether they will bill Medicare. You do not want to have an expensive surgery, only to find out after the fact that the hospital or surgeon has decided not to bill Medicare.

Why would providers not want to use someone's health insurance? Generally, the answer is simple: profit motive. Some hospitals and doctors do not want to accept the contractual discounts or write-offs that health insurance, Medicaid, and Medicare insist on. Instead, they want you to pay them 100 cents on the dollar out of your settlement. They do not care whether you will be left with any money afterwards for pain, disability, or income loss. Some doctor's offices and hospitals, though, actually believe that you cannot use health insurance after a wreck. Even though they are mistaken, it usually takes attorney intervention to correct the problem. *Remember that time is of the essence in this situation.* If providers wait too long to submit bills to health insurance, the submission may be outside of the policy's time limit.

B. Should You Use Your Own Auto Insurance to Pay Your Bills (Medical Payments Coverage)?[1]

The answer to this question is also "yes." Just like health insurance, many people are reluctant to use their own auto insurance to pay medical bills after a wreck. There are generally two reasons for this reluctance: 1) a feeling that you were the innocent party who did nothing wrong and, therefore, it is the other person's insurance company that should pay for everything; and/or 2) a generalized fear that if you use your own insurance, your rates will go up.

If someone else caused a wreck in which you were injured, then *you are the innocent party who did nothing wrong.* However, the other driver's carrier will not pay for your treatment until the case is com-

---

1   The discussion in this section applies to state that do not have "no fault" legislation. In those states, medical payments coverage is generally replaced with the "no fault" coverage.

pletely over with and you have signed a full and final release. So, if you need treatment and want to make a full recovery, something will need to be done about the bills in the meantime.

Additionally, any insurance company that would raise your rates because you used your medical payments coverage due to a wreck that was not your fault is not a company deserving of your business. Every time you make a premium payment, you pay a certain amount to have medical payments coverage (*see* the policy declarations page on the nest page of this book). To pay for something you are afraid to use makes no sense. Medical payments coverage is *designed* for this very purpose. Moreover, your carrier will be *repaid* for this expense out of the settlement, so there simply isn't any reason for your rates to be affected.

Being afraid to use coverage you have paid for is like buying a car from a car dealer that you are afraid to drive off the lot. Instead, you go to the dealer every month and make payments on the car while the car remains on the lot untouched.

Auto insurance is the only business I know of where the sellers have created a climate in which the buyer is afraid to use the product they have purchased. This is especially galling given the fact that in most states, it's a violation of the law to fail to have auto insurance.

Now, let's explain exactly how YOUR auto insurance can help you if you've been in a wreck that was not your fault. In Indiana, as in many other states, each automobile insurance policy contains several different types of coverages: collision, liability, uninsured and underinsured, and medical payments coverage.

The limits of the medical payments coverage will normally not be as high as the liability or the uninsured/underinsured coverage. For instance, the medical payments limits we see most commonly are $1,000, $5,000, or $10,000. This coverage is available to apply toward medical bills for anyone who is in the covered auto and sustains injuries, regardless of fault. If you are injured in someone else's auto, their medical payments will cover you. When their medical payments coverage is exhausted, your medical payments coverage can usually be used in addition to their coverage. If they have no medical payments coverage, then your personal medical payments coverage should apply immediately.

Below is a sample automobile declarations page showing a policy with $5,000 per-person in medical payments coverage. The "Medical Payments" is listed as coverage B on this policy and you can also see the exact amounts of each premium payment that are applied to this coverage.

Western Reserve Group

Western Reserve Mutual Casualty Company ' Lightning Rod Mutual Insurance Company
Sonnenberg Mutual Insurance Company
Wooster, Ohio

PERSONAL AUTO POLICY

WESTERN RESERVE MUTUAL CASUALTY COMPANY	POLICY NUMBER
NAMED INSURED:	
	ACCOUNT #
	EFFECTIVE DATE OF AMENDMENT

NO.	YEAR	MAKE	MODEL	IDENTIFICATION NUMBER	ST/TERR	CLASS	OTC	COLL	SYM	DRIVER ASSIGN
1					IN 116	545020			20	1
2					IN 116	142020			17	2
6					IN 116	218720			16	3 4

NO.	DRIVER	TIER	DATE OF BIRTH	AUTO	NO.	DRIVER	TIER	DATE OF BIRTH	AUTO
1									
2									-

EXCLUDED DRIVERS -

WE INSURE YOU ONLY FOR THE COVERAGES FOR WHICH A PREMIUM & LIMIT OF LIABILITY IS SHOWN BELOW

COVERAGES	LIMIT OF LIABILITY	1	4	6
A. BODILY INJURY LIABILITY				
$ 100,000 EACH PERSON $ 300,000 EACH ACCIDENT		89.00	89.00	173.00
PROPERTY DAMAGE LIABILITY $ 100,000 EACH ACCIDENT		83.00	82.00	160.00
B. MEDICAL PAYMENTS $ 5,000 EACH PERSON		16.00	16.00	39.00
C. UNINSURED/UNDERINSURED MOTORISTS-BI & FULL COV DED. PD		38.00	38.00	38.00
$ 100,000 EA PER $ 300,000 EA ACC $ 100,000 EA ACC				
D. DAMAGE TO YOUR AUTO-DEDUCTIBLE/GLASS DEDUCTIBLE				
OTHER THAN COLLISION 1. 500 4. 500 6. 500		133.00	131.00	273.00
$0 GLASS 1. YES 4. YES 6. YES				
COLLISION 1. 500 4. 500 6. 500		212.00	261.00	533.00
TOWING AND LABOR MAXIMUM LIMIT $ 50 PER CLAIM		6.00	6.00	
TRANS EXP/RENTAL RE. $ 30 PER DAY $ 900 TOTAL		10.00	10.00	
TRANS EXP/RENTAL RE. $ 20 PER DAY $ 600 TOTAL				INCL

TOTAL PREMIUM BY AUTO	587.00	633.00	1,218.00

PREFERRED DISCOUNTS APPLIED:					AUTO SUB TOTAL $ 2,436.00
Renewal Discount	Multi-Car	Good Student	Anti-Lock Brake		ENDORSEMENTS $
Anti-Theft Device	Multi-Policy	Advance Quote	Active Disabling		FULL TERM PREM $ 2,436.00
Passive Restraint					ADDL PREMIUM $
ALTERNATE GARAGING:					RETURN PREMIUM $

THIS IS NOT A BILL / SEE YOUR BILLING STATEMENT

LOSS PAYEE:

COUNTERSIGNED – AUTHORIZED REPRESENTATIVE

THIS DECLARATIONS PAGE WITH PERSONAL AUTO POLICY PROVISIONS OR POLICY JACKET AND PERSONAL AUTO POLICY FORM, TOGETHER WITH
APPLICABLE ENDORSEMENTS, IF ANY, ISSUED TO FORM A PART THEREOF, COMPLETES THE NUMBERED POLICY.

The bottom line is that 1) you are paying for this coverage, 2) it's designed to benefit you if you have been injured in a wreck, and 3) it *will* benefit you if you have been injured in a wreck. So don't be afraid to use it.

C. An Explanation of the Other Coverages on Your Auto Insurance Policy

Although the other coverages on your policy are not necessarily designed to pay your medical bills after a wreck, this seems like a logical place to discuss briefly standard policy coverages that may come into play after a wreck.

What follows is a short explanation of standard coverages available in most auto policies. We will use the Western Reserve declarations page presented above for an Indiana auto policy as an example.

1. What is a Declarations Page?

This is a relatively simple one or two page document that most people keep somewhere in their possession, often in the glove compartment. If the client cannot find their "dec page," their carrier or agent can usually print one off their computer in a matter of seconds.

The declarations page very simply "declares" or states the amount of automobile insurance coverage the client has purchased. Like the Western Reserve policy shown, it may also list the amount you pay each year in premiums for each separate coverage.

2. Bodily Injury Liability

A declarations page is usually the first coverage listed on the declarations page. It is set forth as coverage "A" in the example. This covers people you may injure if you cause a wreck. In this policy there is a maximum coverage of $100,000 per person and $300,000 per accident. This means that if the insured causes a wreck, the most Western Reserve will pay any one person (or that person's estate if they die in the wreck) is $100,000. Even if the person is paralyzed and has $500,000 in medical bills, Western Reserve will only pay them $100,000 because that is the coverage limit that was paid for. The most Western Reserve will pay, total, for any one wreck, no matter how many people are injured or how severe their injuries, is $300,000.

3. Uninsured/Underinsured Motorist Coverage

Because we have already discussed coverage "B" (medical payments), we will skip ahead to coverage "C," as listed in the Western Reserve policy. *This is perhaps the most important, and most often overlooked, coverage in every auto policy.* The dollar amount of this coverage usually tracks (i.e., is the same as) coverage A, the liability coverage. Uninsured and underinsured motorist coverages are separate and different coverages; yet they are also similar coverages and, consequently, are usually listed together and have the same coverage limits. The key to these coverages is that they are for your benefit, and if you need them, you will REALLY NEED THEM.

Uninsured motorist coverage is generally for a) you, b) anyone in your vehicle and c) your family members to use in case any of you are injured in a wreck caused by someone who has no auto liability coverage (i.e., someone who is "uninsured" and operating their vehicle in violation of most state laws).

There are a surprisingly high number of drivers on our roads who have absolutely no auto insurance. In fact, according to a USA Today article in 2011, **one out of every seven drivers on our roads has no insurance.**[2]

If you are hit and injured by someone with no auto insurance, your insurance carrier is supposed to stand in the shoes of that uninsured

---

2 "One in Seven Drivers Have No Insurance," by Larry Copeland, September 12, 2011 (emphasis added); http://usatoday30.usatoday.com/news/nation/story/2011-09-11/uninsured-drivers/50363390/1

driver and pay you whatever compensation the uninsured driver is legally obligated to pay you. This may include medical bills, lost income, and pain and suffering. *Understand, however, that even though they are your auto insurance company, they will not treat you any differently than a stranger off the street. They are, for all intents and purposes, your adversary and will do their best to minimize the claim.* **If you find yourself in this situation, hire a good and experienced personal injury attorney.**

Underinsured motorist coverage is generally for a) you, b) anyone in your vehicle, and c) your family members to use in case any of you are injured in a wreck caused by someone who has insufficient auto liability coverage to compensate you for your personal injury claim. *If you ever need this coverage, you definitely need an attorney!* There are rules that apply to the use of this coverage that you must follow in order to be eligible for the coverage. If you do not follow the rules, you may not be able to use the coverage. The most critical thing that must happen before you can use this coverage is that you must first be offered the entire policy limit of the person who caused the wreck. *In Indiana, though, you cannot accept that offer and preserve your right to receive underinsured motorist benefits unless you follow certain procedural guidelines.*

If possible, we recommend purchasing an umbrella to go over and above the coverages outlined in the Western Reserve policy. Most umbrella coverages will act, not only as additional liability coverage, but also as additional uninsured and underinsured motorist coverages. Many folks are surprised by the affordability of this coverage. According to *Car and Driver,* in 2009 a $1,000,000 umbrella could be purchased for between $150 and $300 per year.[3] And, the next million above that may be half that much! Not a lot to pay if you are hit and severely injured by someone with no insurance, or someone with only $25,000 per-person liability limits.

---

3   http://www.caranddriver.com/reviews/should-i-purchase-an-umbrella-liability-policy-info.

4. <u>Collision Coverage (Damage to Your Auto)</u>

This is coverage "D" listed in the Western Reserve policy. It covers damage to your vehicle. This is the coverage many people drop when they are driving an older auto that they don't intend to repair if it's wrecked.

If you are in a wreck that is someone else's fault and their insurance company is dragging their feet assessing and repairing your vehicle, don't be afraid to call your company and use your collision coverage. The other person's carrier will have to repay your carrier and pay you your deductible. Also, if your vehicle is totaled and the other person's carrier isn't offering a fair price, check with your carrier to see if they will give you a better deal. It costs nothing to explore this option. Again, don't be afraid to use the coverage you have paid for.

Because property damages issues are often critical and time sensitive, pick an attorney that has a person in their office who can assist you with their property damage claims. Some law firms, like ours, do not charge for this service.

Finally, remember that even if your property damage claim is handled quickly and satisfactorily by the other driver's carrier, that does *not* mean that your injury claim will be as easy.

5. <u>Gap Coverage</u>

The last coverage we will discuss is called "gap" coverage and is not represented in the Western Reserve declarations page. Gap coverage is recommended for anyone who a) buys a new car and finances it, b) leases a car, or 3) purchases a used vehicle at a cut-rate dealer and finances the vehicle in such a way that more is owed on the vehicle than the vehicle is worth.

In all of the above-listed situations, the purchaser will drive off the car lot in what is called an "upside down" position. In other words, they will owe their lender more than the vehicle is worth. If that person runs into a tree on the way home from the dealer and totals their vehicle, they may actually have to pay their bank or loan company more on their loan than their vehicle is worth. Therefore, this unlucky person will owe their bank or loan company additional funds even after the insurance carrier pays an amount equal to the vehicle's fair market value.

Insurance companies are only legally responsible for paying you the fair market value of your vehicle. If you owe more on the vehicle than it's worth on the open market, they do not have to pay you the difference.

Gap coverage is not expensive and shrinks along with the "gap" between the loan amount and the fair market value of the vehicle until the coverage finally disappears (if you own the vehicle long enough).

D. <u>What to Do if You Have No Health Insurance or Medical Payments Coverage?</u>

Unfortunately, the reality in today's world is that many hard-working people have no health insurance. These same folks often purchase cut-rate auto insurance from carriers like Safe Auto and have no medical payments coverage. Because the insurance carrier for the person who caused the wreck will refuse to pay their bills, these people are in an immediate bind after a wreck. If they are living "pay check to pay check" and missing work due to their injuries, their problems are further compounded. They risk irreparable damage to a credit rating that may already be shaky.

People who have no way to pay their medical bills after a wreck should seek an immediate consultation with a good personal injury attorney. Working with an attorney who has a reputation for paying all of his client's medical bills after a settlement and has a good working relationship with many hospitals and other medical providers can be a lifesaver. The law firm will contact the unpaid providers and advise them of their representation. They will let them know that the wreck was not the client's fault. The lawyers will tell the providers that if they will refrain from harassing the client for immediate payment and refrain from turning them over to a collection agency, the lawyers will make sure the bills are paid out of any settlement or jury verdict. There are also some health care providers who will provide future treatment as long as the lawyer promises to pay them when a resolution is reached.

VII. SOFT TISSUE INJURY TREATMENT AFTER A WRECK

Medical treatment of soft tissue injuries following a wreck varies greatly. People are often confused about what type of treatment they should have after a wreck and what type of health care provider is best at treating soft tissue injuries. Here is some helpful information about the different types of treatment available and the different health care providers who treat soft tissue injuries.

A. What Happens in the Emergency Room?

It's always a good idea to go to the emergency room after a car wreck if you have pain, feel strange, or believe that you have been injured (remember that what feels like minor pain often evolves into a more serious problem once the adrenaline wears off). However, keep in mind that the emergency room's first priority is to make sure you do not have a major or life-threatening problem. Therefore, if you hit your head, they may do a CT scan to make sure you do not have bleeding in your brain. And if you have a lot of neck or back pain, they may do X-rays to make sure there is no fracture that could cause spinal instability. If these tests are negative, however, that does not mean you are uninjured. It may simply mean that you have a soft tissue injury that cannot be visualized on these tests.

Also, understand that emergency rooms do not "treat" soft tissue injuries after car wrecks. They may prescribe pain medication or muscle relaxers, but this is not really treatment, and often does not "cure" the problem.

B. Where to Go After the Emergency Room?

Many times, the emergency room doctor will note in the medical records that the patient was told to "follow up with their family doctor if symptoms persist," or "follow up in several days." If you are not fine within a week of the wreck, it's critical to get in to see someone who is experienced in treating soft tissue injuries as soon as possible.

So, where do you go after the emergency room? Or, if you didn't go to the emergency room, where do you go for your initial medical treatment. You have several options. Usually you should start with a family doctor, a chiropractor, an osteopath, or a physiatrist.

1. Family Physician

Although there are several treatment options for people with soft tissue injuries, many folks choose to see their family physician. This may be because they were told by the emergency room to follow up with their family doctor. It may be because the client's health insurance requires them to go through the family doctor. Or, it may be because they really like and trust the family doctor.

The family practitioner, however, often is not a specialist in treating soft tissue injuries. He or she can refer you for physical therapy, or refer you to a specialist, or prescribe medication, or even order an MRI. But the actual *treatment* of a soft tissue injury will usually be performed by someone else. The family doctor, though, can manage the referrals and monitor your progress. But be leery of the family doctor who just wants to prescribe pain medicine but fails to recommend treatment that helps you get better.

The important thing is to get in to see someone who can help as soon as possible. Waiting three weeks for an appointment after a wreck is never a good idea.

2. Chiropractor

Chiropractors specialize in helping people heal after suffering soft tissue injuries. Therefore, chiropractic treatment can be an excellent choice of care after a wreck.

These days, chiropractic care is a well-accepted and "mainstream" way to treat soft tissue injuries. Many family doctors and orthopedic surgeons will refer patients to chiropractors for treatment. A growing number of chiropractic offices can provide the same physical therapy modalities and treatment as a hospital therapy department while also having the advantage of providing chiropractic adjustments and other chiropractic techniques to speed healing. Many chiropractors have the capability to perform X-rays in their offices. Moreover, the insurance carriers have gradually come to accept chiropractic treatment as a legitimate and helpful form of treatment for a soft tissue injury.

Chiropractors do not, and cannot, prescribe narcotic pain medication. Therefore, they are dealing with the patient's injury and trying to fix it, rather than using medication that may simply mask the problem. Some injured people take pain medicine prescribed in the emergency room only to find that once the prescription runs out, the injury is still there. Although they were simply following the orders of the emergency room doctor, they may have been better off actually seeking *treatment* for their injury at an earlier date.

There are several other advantages to obtaining chiropractic care after suffering a soft tissue injury. First, chiropractors often have more flexible hours than doctors and physical therapists. For example, many chiropractic offices stay open for evening hours. Other chiropractors are closed one day during the week so that they can be open on Saturdays. Second, you do not need a referral or a prescription to see a chiropractor. Just call and make an appointment. Third, chiropractic treatment is often less expensive than formal physical therapy. Fourth, you will find that many chiropractors and their staff have a genuine interest in helping you and making sure that you are satisfied with their services. They want you to go back out into the community and recommend them. While hospital therapy departments get their referrals from doctors, chiropractors often rely on word of mouth for their clientele. Fifth, as mentioned above, chiropractors are specialists in soft tissue injury treatment and often attend advanced seminars where the latest knowledge and auto accident and injury treatment techniques are discussed. Many chiropractors have gained extensive experience over time at diagnosing and assisting patients who have been involved in automobile wrecks.

Here is a more formal definition of chiropractic as given by the American Chiropractic Association:

> Chiropractic is a health care profession that focuses on disorders of the musculoskeletal system and the nervous system, and the effects of these disorders on general health. Chiropractic care is used most often to treat neuromusculoskeletal complaints, including but not limited to back pain, neck pain, pain in the joints of the arms or legs, and headaches.

> Doctors of Chiropractic – often referred to as chiropractors or chiropractic physicians – practice a drug-free, hands-on approach to health care that includes patient examination, diagnosis and treatment. Chiropractors have broad diagnostic skills and are also trained to recommend therapeutic and rehabilitative exercises, as well as to provide nutritional, dietary and lifestyle counseling.[1]

3. Osteopath

An osteopath is, in some ways, like a cross between an MD and a chiropractor. They often perform osteopathic manipulations like a chiropractor, but an osteopath can also prescribe medication and even perform injections and surgeries. An osteopath is not an MD; he or she is a DO (i.e., doctor of osteopathy).

> Osteopathic medicine is a distinct form of medical practice in the United States. Osteopathic medicine provides all of the benefits of modern medicine including prescription drugs, surgery, and the use of technology to diagnose disease and evaluate injury. It also offers the added benefit of hands-on diagnosis and treatment through a system of therapy known as osteopathic manipulative medicine. Osteopathic medicine emphasizes helping each person achieve a high level of wellness by focusing on health promotion and disease prevention.

> Osteopathic physicians, also known as DOs, work in partnership with their patients. They consider the impact that lifestyle and community have on the health of each individual, and

---

1   http://www.acatoday.org/level2_css.cfm?T1ID=13&T2ID=61

they work to break down barriers to good health. DOs are licensed to practice the full scope of medicine in all 50 states. They practice in all types of environments, including the military, and in all types of specialties, from family medicine to obstetrics, surgery, and aerospace medicine.

DOs are trained to look at the whole person from their first days of medical school, which means they see each person as more than just a collection of organ systems and body parts that may become injured or diseased. This holistic approach to patient care means that osteopathic medical students learn how to integrate the patient into the health care process as a partner. They are trained to communicate with people from diverse backgrounds, and they get the opportunity to practice these skills in their classrooms and learning laboratories, frequently with standardized and simulated patients. [2]

4. <u>Physical Medicine and Rehabilitation Specialist ("Physiatrist")</u>

A physical medicine and rehabilitation specialist is like a cross between a general practitioner and an orthopedic surgeon. They generally do not perform surgeries; however, they often do minor surgical procedures like epidural injections. They also perform trigger point and steroid injections. Most people who have some form of soft tissue injury are better off seeing a physiatrist than an orthopedic surgeon. They are better equipped to deal with this type of injury. If a physiatrist feels surgery is indicated, they will refer to a surgeon.

Many physiatrists also utilize "alternative" forms of medicine, such as acupuncture and relaxation techniques, to treat pain.

According to the American Academy of Physical Medicine and Rehabilitation,

A physiatrist, or rehabilitation physician, is a medical doctor who has also completed residency training in the medi-

2   American Association of Colleges of Osteopathic Medicine Website: http://www.aacom.org/about/osteomed/pages/default.aspx

cal specialty of physical medicine and rehabilitation (PM&R). This physician is a nerve, muscle, bone and brain expert who diagnoses and treats injuries or illnesses that affect how you move. The physiatric approach to patient care looks at the whole person and not just one symptom or condition. Rehabilitation physicians do not perform surgery.[3]

The American Academy of Physical Medicine and Rehabilitation is a national medical specialty organization that represents over 8,000 physical medicine and rehabilitation physicians.

5. Pain Management Specialist

A pain management specialist can be a physician or an osteopath who specializes in treating pain. The specialty of pain management cuts across, and overlaps with, other specialties. However, a pain management specialist can often be the last resort for folks with injuries that do not respond to any form of treatment and can only be "managed" with pain medication (often narcotic) or electronic stimulation devices that interrupt the body's pain pathways.

The American Academy of Pain Management states as follows about their organization, which helps explain more about the specialty.

The Academy is a nonprofit professional organization serving clinicians, representing a broad number of disciplines, who treat people with pain. Founded in 1988, the Academy is the largest pain management organization in the nation and the only one that embraces an integrative model of care, which is patient-centered, focuses on the "whole" person, is informed by evidence, and brings together, all appropriate therapeutic approaches to reduce pain and achieve optimal health and healing. [4]

---

3 AAPM&R Website: http://www.aapmr.org/patients/Pages/default.aspx

4 American Academy of Pain Management website: http://www.aapainmanage.org/aboutus/Welcome.php

6. <u>Orthopedic Surgeon</u>

Orthopedic surgeons do wonderful things to assist and fix people with broken bones, degenerated joints, herniated discs, and severely damaged spines. Orthopedic surgeons, however, are not necessarily the best practitioners to treat soft tissue injuries. If you are not a surgical candidate, an orthopedic surgeon will often refer you for physical therapy. Any of the other practitioners mentioned above (including chiropractors) can do this. These other practitioners will often have much more to offer you in the way of therapies and alternative treatments that will allow you to have the best chance of a full recovery. While orthopedic surgeons also perform injections which can be very helpful in certain situations, the orthopedic surgeon's ultimate form of therapy is surgery. If surgery won't benefit you, a good orthopedic surgeon will refer you to other practitioners who can do more for you.

7. <u>Neurologist</u>

Sometimes people with severe soft tissue injuries are referred to a neurologist. A neurologist is usually defined as a physician who treats diseases of the central nervous system.[5] Neurologists do not perform surgery; however, they do perform electronic testing, such as EMGs and nerve conduction studies to determine if you have a nerve that is being impinged upon due to a neck or back injury. If you do have such an impingement, you may be a surgical candidate and they will refer you to a surgeon.

8. <u>Neurosurgeon</u>

A neurosurgeon can be defined as "a surgeon [who] specializes in managing diseases of the brain, spine and peripheral nerves."[6] Neurosurgeons and orthopedic surgeons both perform surgeries on the spine. However, there is generally no reason for someone to see a neurosurgeon for a soft tissue injury. In fact, no one will even suggest it, unless they believe you are a surgical candidate.

5   http://www.merriam-webster.com/dictionary/neurologist; *Mosby's Medical Dictionary, 8th edition.* © 2009.

6   *McGraw-Hill Concise Dictionary of Modern Medicine.* © 2002 by The McGraw-Hill Companies, Inc.

9. **Dentist / Facial Pain Specialist / Oral Maxillofacial Surgeon**

As discussed in Chapter V, Section D of this book, injuries to the jaw can occur in what seem like relatively minor car crashes. The jaw can be injured even if the person does not strike their head on anything inside the vehicle. Dentists are familiar with the symptoms of temporomandibular joint injuries. And certainly seeing a dentist can be a logical first step when someone thinks they may have a jaw injury after a wreck. However, most dentists are not equipped to treat dysfunction of the temporomandibular joint effectively. Most dentists are not trained in the diagnosis and treatment of soft tissue injuries of the head and neck. Their training is specialized in the field of teeth and gum issues.

Instead, due to the technical nature of the temporomandibular joint treatment regime, it is usually necessary to see a TMJ specialist or a facial pain specialist.[7]

> Traditionally [temporomandibular disfunction] treatment is divided into two phases: phase I and phase II. Phase I includes all techniques designed for pain reduction and restoring the TMJs to a state of quiescence. Phase II corrects any discrepancies between mandibular position, teeth, and supporting structures. This is often considered the dental aspect of TMD treatment.[8]

Phase II treatment can involve the use of custom-made orthodontics (i.e., plastic mouthpieces). In severe cases, it may be necessary to consult with an oral maxillofacial surgeon[9] and even undergo surgery.

---

7 See the website of the American Academy of Craniofacial Pain: http://www.aacfp.org/

8 *Soft Tissue Injuries: Diagnosis and Treatment,* Hanley & Belfus, Inc. (1998) Edited by Windsor and Lox, "Temporomandibular Joint Dysfunction," by Christopher R. Brown, DDS, MPS, p. 238.

9 http://www.aaoms.org/tmj.php

10. <u>Physical Therapist</u>

Physical therapists are licensed health care professionals who work with patients with a variety of illnesses, injuries, and post-surgical conditions. The American Academy of Physical Therapists has produced a document entitled *Today's Physical Therapist: A Comprehensive Review of A 21st Century Health Care Profession*. The document can be accessed on line.[10] The document was created to "provide accurate information for government entities and the public about the history, role, educational preparation, laws governing practice, standards of practice, evidence base of the profession, payment for physical therapy services, and workforce issues unique to the physical therapy profession."[11]

The American Physical Therapy Association provides the following description of the physical therapist's role in patient/client management:

> Physical Therapists provide care to patients/clients of all ages who have impairments, activity limitations, and participation restrictions due to musculoskeletal, neuromuscular, cardiovascular/pulmonary, and/or integumentary disorders. Following the patient/client management model ...physical therapists design individualized plans of care based on their clinical judgment and patient/client goals. Physical therapists collaborate with other health care professionals to address patient needs, increase communication, and provide efficient and effective care across the continuum of health care settings.[12]

Physical therapists can be extremely helpful in treating soft tissue injuries. Three to six weeks of physical therapy is the traditional, and often initial, treatment prescribed by many physicians to assist soft tissue injury victims. Physical therapists use massage, stretching, and strengthening exercises along with hot, cold, ultrasound, and electric stimulation therapies to treat soft tissues. Minor injuries can sometimes be successfully treated and resolved with such treatment. However, more

---

10   http://www.apta.org/uploadedFiles/APTAorg/Practice_and_Patient_Care/PR_
and_Marketing/Market_to_Professionals/TodaysPhysicalTherapist.pdf
11   Id.
12   Id. At p. 9

complicated soft tissue injuries may improve, but not entirely resolve, even after several rounds of physical therapy.

Many chiropractic clinics now employ licensed physical therapists. Consequently, clients who treat with these clinics can often receive chiropractic adjustments and other chiropractic treatments while also being treated by licensed physical therapists.

11. Massage Therapist

"Massage therapy is one of the oldest health care practices known to history. References to massage are found in Chinese medical texts more than 4,000 years old."[13]

> Massage therapy is the scientific manipulation of the soft tissues of the body for the purpose of normalizing those tissues and consists of manual techniques that include applying fixed or movable pressure, holding, and/or causing movement of or to the body.
>
> Generally, massage is known to affect the circulation of blood and the flow of blood and lymph, reduce muscular tension or flaccidity, affect the nervous system through stimulation or sedation, and enhance tissue healing. These effects provide a number of benefits...[14]

Remember, many chiropractors have massage therapists that work in their offices, and virtually every physical therapy center will also have licensed massage therapists. There are apparently wide differences between states and even cities regarding licensing requirements. This is something that has created difficulties for the American Massage Therapy Association and their members.[15]

---

13   *The Free Medical Dictionary* by Farlex; http://medical-dictionary. thefreedictionary.com/massage+therapy.

14   Id.

15   http://www.amtamassage.org/uploads/cms/documents/gr_overview.pdf

12. Urgent Care Centers

There has been a proliferation of urgent care centers over the last several years. These are places where people can go for acute injuries and illness and see a physician without an appointment. The Urgent Care Association of America states the following on their website:

> Urgent care centers provide walk-in, extended hour access for acute illness and injury care that is either beyond the scope or availability of the typical primary care practice or retail clinic. There are over 8,700 urgent care centers in the US, approximately 4,500 of which are fully-fledged centers that would meet the criteria for a Certified Urgent Care center.

> UCAOA now provides specific criteria for defining what an urgent care center is. Urgent care centers have a broader and deeper scope of services than retail clinics, but are not equivalent to emergency departments. Urgent care ideally helps in reserving the nation's emergency room resources for more serious, life-threatening conditions.

> Urgent care helps to improve both access to care and proper utilization of health system resources. There are many studies by the CDC and others that identify significant numbers of patients who went to an ER that could have been treated in urgent care centers. *(UCAOA does recommend that all patients who believe they may have a life threatening condition seek care in an emergency facility.)*

> The ability of an urgent care center to provide immediate care for acute, non-life threatening illness and injury is a critical component of any community's health system. Cooperation between patients, primary physicians, emergency departments and urgent care providers can create a network of care options that puts the patient in the right hands at the right time for the right level of care.[16]

Many of our clients have sought treatment at urgent care centers after wrecks. These are normally clients who did not go by ambulance to

---

16   http://www.ucaoa.org/index.php

the hospital from the scene of the wreck, but began having pain within several days and sought treatment. Often clients who seek urgent care treatment do not have established primary care physicians or family doctors. Sometimes, however, clients go to urgent care centers because they do not want to wait a week or two to get in to their family doctor for an appointment.

Clients normally receive very good treatment at urgent care centers and the physicians and employees at these centers are easy to work with. However, while urgent care physicians might prescribe treatment such as therapy, urgent care centers do not provide therapy or treatment and are not a substitute for a physician or chiropractor who can follow the patient's progress. That is not what urgent care centers are designed for.

C. What to Consider if Chiropractic or Traditional Physical Therapy Do Not Cure Your Soft Tissue Injury

If chiropractic treatment and/or physical therapy do not resolve your soft tissue injury symptoms, then talk to your chiropractor or physician about seeing someone else and trying some additional form of treatment. A physiatrist or osteopath may be a next logical step. Injections, different types of therapy, and even alternative forms of treatment such as acupuncture, can be very helpful.

Unfortunately, soft tissue injuries that appear to be similar in nature often seem to react differently to the same treatment. In other words, while most simple forearm fractures may react similarly to being put in a cast for five weeks, the same is not necessarily true with soft tissue neck injuries. The severity of the soft tissue injury, the amount of pre-existing arthritis, the injured person's job, the person's muscle tone, etc. can all factor into the amount of treatment and the kind of treatment needed to relieve the problem. This is simply due to physics and the nature of the human body.

In my experience, insurance carriers feel an irresistible urge to apply a mathematical formula to everything—including medical treatment for soft tissue injuries. If you are a janitor and have a fractured forearm, an insurance company might say, "OK, it's reasonable for that particular injury to be put in a cast for five weeks and for you to miss six weeks of work." In 90% of cases, they may be right and thus a simple bone fracture might be susceptible to this kind of formula. The problems come when carriers try to apply the same strict formulas to soft tissue injuries from wrecks. And believe me—that's *exactly* what they do.

Insurance companies attempt to apply formulas to soft tissue injuries every day. They will attempt to allow a limited number of chiropractic treatments, they will tell you that all soft tissue injuries are healed in two to three months, they will say that if there is only x amount of damage to your car, there can only be x amount of damage to your body, and on and on. Carriers will sometimes even contend that if your treatment does not conform to their pre-conceived formula, you must be trying to defraud them.

The truth is that each case is different and each person's soft tissue structure reacts differently, even if the force applied should happen to be exactly the same. Whether it takes you 30 days or 180 days to recover fully from a soft tissue injury will depend on many factors, and some of those factors are out of your control. And, if you are one of the unlucky few, you might have some degree of pain for the rest of your life as a result of a soft tissue injury. If that happens, instead of assisting you, the insurance companies will question your honesty.

D. Can Soft Tissue Injuries Be Permanent?

Soft tissue injuries can cause long-term and even permanent problems. However, you will find insurance adjusters and doctors (who are hired by insurance adjusters) that may state that there is no such thing as a "permanent" soft tissue injury. They will say that, by definition, a soft tissue injury, like a bruise, will automatically resolve over time. There are many more medical practitioners who view soft tissue injuries as something that can potentially cause long-term, permanent, or chronic problems.

Unlike a simple fracture of a bone, it is believed that soft tissues do not necessarily "knit" back together in a perfect union that is just as strong and functional as before the injury. Many chiropractors, osteopaths, and physiatrists believe that some soft tissues that are stretched and torn do not return to normal length. They believe that some tissues that are torn, while they may "knit" back together, will do so in a different fashion than pre-injury.

The following excerpt from a paper published by the South African Spine Society regarding "whiplash neck injury" summarizes fairly well the various opinions relating to the potential permanence of soft tissue injuries of the neck:

- In contrast to fractures of bone, which once healed typically recover to normal strength, alignment, and function; sprains or disruptions of soft tissues always result in some degree of permanent weakening and may result in some degree of permanent lengthening of the injured soft tissue structures.

- A neck which has "recovered" from a whiplash injury may withstand the strains and loads placed upon it for the rest of the individual's life by the individual's normal work and recreational activities, but it may not. Many fortunate individuals do manage to return to their previous activities and never experience any further neck symptoms or limitations. In these cases the recovery is equivalent to "cure."

- In other less fortunate cases, where full resolution of symptoms and apparent resolution of limitations has occurred, the resumption of previous activities and postures leads to secondary deterioration at some later stage in the individual's life.

- Whether a "recovered" neck will remain asymptomatic and fully functional or not can unfortunately not be predicted or guaranteed in any given case, as the ability or failure in this regard is a function of the degree of injury and permanent damage [not measurable by any reliable scientific device] on the one hand, and the nature, degree and repetitiveness of strain applied to the neck of the individual on the other.

- For the above reasons it is wise to apply sensible personal neck care and protection in the long term, even following injuries which appear to have "recovered." In essence this concept means to: · apply those adaptations to posture, ergonomics, etc. which will not impair one's productivity or prevent essential activities, · avoid unimportant activities and positions that are known to strain the neck, and · spare one's neck for the important things in life.

- Unfortunately a certain number of individuals who have suffered whiplash neck injury fail to recover, and continue to experience symptoms and functional impairment in the long term.

- In these cases, where medical science in general, or the treating health care professionals individually, are considered to have failed the patient, secondary psychological sequelae are inevitable.

- It is often not possible to identify particular reasons why a particular individual has failed to recover, except in the case of severe or complicated injuries where permanent problems are more likely.

- Chronic symptoms and functional impairment typically result in a reduction or cessation of sporting, recreational, and other nonessential activities.

- In a smaller number of chronic sufferers the complex syndrome results in a degree of occupational disability, usually by way of a reduction in productivity, and sometimes even in premature retirement from work.[1]

---

1   The South African Spine Society: Whiplash Neck Injuries, http://www.saspine. org/conditions/whiplash_neck_injury.htm.

VIII. THE "DIFFICULTIES" WITH MANY SOFT-TISSUE INJURY CASES

What follows is a list of generally perceived difficulties and stumbling blocks that many people (and lawyers) encounter when managing and ultimately attempting to resolve soft tissue injury claims.

A. "Minor" Vehicle Damage (Does it Equal Minor Injury?)

The issue most often seized upon by insurance adjusters to minimize a claimant's injuries is lack of serious damage to the injured person's vehicle. *Although most adjusters and all insurance carriers now know that **there is no direct correlation between damage to a vehicle and damage to a body**, that knowledge will not slow them down or prevent them in any way from trying to convince an injured person that no one will believe they are hurt if their vehicle damage is not impressive.* This plays right into the injured person's guilt complex (see Chapter II, Section B of this book).

As discussed earlier in this book, minor impact soft tissue ("MIST") cases have been a target for insurance carriers since at least the early 1990s. These are the cases every insurance carrier wants to "lowball." The carriers would like us all to believe that it is virtually impossible to sustain a permanent, serious injury in a low-damage car crash and, therefore, these claims should be handled differently. Because there are a very large number of MIST cases, singling out MIST cases for "special" treatment was one of the hallmarks of McKinsey's recommendation to Allstate as a way to drive profits in the claims arena.

The simplicity of looking at minor vehicle damage and somehow equating it to damage to the occupants is very appealing to insurance carriers and defense lawyers. They know that a large percent of the public is susceptible to the unsophisticated formula of: LITTLE DAMAGE = LITTLE INJURY. To many folks, this equation just seems like common sense, but the scientific community has known better for a very long time.

As far back as 1955, [Derwin] Severy discussed the low speed impact dilemma. "The low speed impact is very common in the urban automobile collisions and may be the most misleading ...Unlike most types of collisions, the rear-end collision frequently results in minor vehicle damage with major bodily injury ...Frequently, he is not immediately aware that he has suffered an injury which may require weeks or months for recovery." Even today we find the "low speed impact" having minor if no outside visible damage to the vehicle yet the "victim" has reported or documented disabling and sometimes non-reversible injuries.[2]

In 1997, British forensic engineer, Malcolm Robbins, wrote an article copyrighted by the Society of Automotive Engineers entitled "Lack of Relationship Between Vehicle Damage and Occupant Injury."[3] The abstract of that article states as follows:

A common misconception formulated is that the amount of vehicle crash damage due to a collision, offers a direct correlation to the degree of occupant injury. This paper explores this concept and explains why it is *false reasoning*.[4] Explanations with supporting data are set forth to show how minor vehicle damage can relate or even be the major contributing factor to occupant injury. Mathematical equations and models also support these findings.

In 2005, Christopher Centino, MD, Michael Freeman, PhD and Whitney Elkins, MPH, published an article in the Journal of the Canadian Pain Society entitled "A Review of the Literature Refuting the Concept of Minor

---

2 "Damage and/or Impact Absorber (Isolator) Movements Observed in Low Speed Crash Tests Involving Ford Escorts," R. Malmsbury, J. Eubanks, SAE Technical Paper 940912 (1994), doi:10.4271/940912, p.221, citing "Controlled Automobile Rear-End Collisions, An Investigation of Related Engineering and Medical Phenomena," by Derwin Severy, J. Mathewson, C. Bechtol, Canadian Services Medical Journal (1955).
3 "Lack of Relationship Between Vehicle Damage and Occupant Injury," M. Robbins, SAE Technical Paper 970494 (1997) doi: 10.4271/970494.
4 Emphasis supplied by ME!

Impact Soft Tissue Injury [MIST]."[5] This article contains a review of the literature published over the last 25 years and concludes by stating that

> [w]hile many authors have published studies that would seem to support the MIST hypothesis, the vast majority of work published in the last 10 years would not support MIST.[6]

In fact, there are 63 different references listed in the article. It is, therefore, a great tool for even experienced attorneys to have in their arsenal.

Very simply—

> YOU CANNOT DETERMINE THE EXTENT OF A PERSON'S INJURIES IN [A MOTOR VEHICLE ACCIDENT] BY THE AMOUNT OF MONEY IT TAKES TO REPAIR THE INVOLVED AUTOMOBILES.[7]

Yet virtually every day in the United States, hundreds (or thousands) of soft tissue injury claims are still being evaluated by insurance companies using vehicle damage—or lack thereof—as a large factor in the claim review process. I believe this is still happening because public perception, fueled by the insurance carriers, has lagged behind the science. In other words, many people still believe that you cannot be injured in a vehicle that has sustained only minimal damage. Although this belief is clearly wrong, the carriers profit by perpetuating the myth.

Because perception is often still different from reality on this issue, insurance carriers are able to continue to convince jurors, attorneys, and even injured people that you can't be injured, or injured badly, in a minimal damage wreck. The insurance companies have actively fostered this misconception through their TV commercials and public statements and made it one of the hallmarks of the insurance industry's campaign to reduce claims payments. Alleging that faking injuries and "swoop and squat" (*see* Allstate commercials) schemes are running rampant in our society creates the impression that everyone who claims an injury after a

---

5   Pain Res Manag, 2005 Summer; 10(2): p. 71, Pain Research & Management: The Journal of the Canadian Pain Society.

6   Id.

7   *Factors Which Influence Soft Tissue Injuries in Low Impact Rear End Motor Vehicle Accidents*, Christopher R. Brown DDS, MPS, 1997, Vol. I, p. 82.

minimum damage car wreck is a faker, or is making a "mountain out of a mole hill." This allows insurance adjusters to subtly pressure injured people who are not represented by an attorney to feel guilty about their "alleged" injury. These folks may be more willing to settle their claims quickly and cheaply to avoid being held up to the public ridicule of being someone who "walks around with a neck brace after a minor accident and wants to sue everyone." After all, these are the people who are the butt of late night comedy routines and the targets of conservative politicians and pundits everywhere.

Just because some people who are involved in minor damage wrecks may not be injured (or may be injured very slightly) does not mean that it is impossible to be injured (or injured badly) in a low damage wreck. Or, to put it differently, even if some people are uninjured, it does not follow that everyone must be uninjured. So, even though the cases that find their way to law offices may be the unlucky minority, they are still real cases with real injuries. The insurance companies on the other side of those cases often want to make sweeping generalizations about the person's injuries based only on how their car looked after impact, or based on the fact that the "majority" of people in wrecks with the same dollar amount of property damage are not injured. This is clearly unfair.

It is unfair to generalize about injuries based simply on vehicle damage because there are too many variables at work in each collision. Simply analyzing the cost to repair a vehicle ignores many more relevant factors. Indeed, there are too many important factors and considerations to list them all in this book. Just a few of the factors are 1) vehicle weight, 2) stiffness of frame and bumper, 3) body type and size, 4) whether the person was looking to the side or straight ahead at impact, and 5) the occupants' age and the existence of pre-existing conditions, such as arthritis, etc.[8]

What about some everyday analogies that demonstrate the lack of correlation between property damage and bodily injury?

---

8   "The Effects of Seated Position on Occupant Kinematics in Low Speed Rear-End Impacts," by O. Keifer, P. Layson, B. Reckamp (2005) SAE Technical Paper 2005-01-1204, doi: 10.4271/2006-01-1204; "Injury Rates for Older and Younger Belted drivers in Traffic Accidents," by D. Otte and B. Wiese (2012), SAE Int. J. Passeng. Cars – Mech. Syst. 5(1):506-516, doi: 10.4271/2012-01-0573.

> If a person ran as fast as they could, lowered their head and smashed head-first into a brick wall—would you say that they could not have been injured simply because the brick wall was undamaged (except for possibly a blood stain)?[9]

> Do we say that modern day football players did not sustain concussions and other more serious head injuries simply because, after the collision, their helmets look absolutely perfect (other than perhaps some paint transfer)?[10]

Luckily, there are also a large number of scientific studies and articles in addition to those already cited which support the contention that there is no correlation between bodily injury and vehicle damage. While I do not intend for this book to be a comprehensive listing of such studies and articles, it can serve as a basic resource.

A great repository for articles supporting the fact that minor vehicle damage does not equate to minor bodily injury is the Society of Automobile Engineers (SAE). You can search for and purchase the articles online. SAE has a large variety of published articles discussing this subject, some of which can be summarized as follows:

- Unlike most types of collisions, the REMVA (rear end motor vehicle accident) frequently results in minor vehicle damage with major bodily injury. Frequently the occupant is not immediately aware that an injury has been suffered and may require weeks or months for recovery. The low speed impact may have minor if no outside visible damage to the vehicle, yet the victim documented disabling and sometimes non-reversible injuries.[11]

- "It is ...shown that certain vehicles can sustain significant front or rear impacts without sustaining damage." Moreover, despite an absence of damage in many rear-end collisions, some occu-

9   Borrowed with permission from *Factors Which Influence Soft Tissue Injuries in Low Impact Rear End Motor Vehicle Accidents*, p. 82 by Christopher R. Brown, DDS, MPS.
74   "Damage and/or Impact Absorber (Isolator) Movements Observed in Low Speed Crash Tests Involving Ford Escorts," R. Malmsbury, J. Eubanks, SAE Technical Paper 940912 (1994), doi:10.4271/940912, p.221.

pants experience a consistent pattern of physical symptoms. These are most commonly: pain in the neck, shoulders, arms, occipital headaches, blurred vision, dizziness, and weakness in the upper extremities.[12]

- Bumpers are not designed to protect occupants of vehicles. The purpose of bumper design standards "is to protect the vehicle from costly damage and ensure that the basic vehicle function and safety equipment remain undamaged in low speed impacts."[13]

- "In very low speed crashes, advanced age, stenosis and degeneration of the cervical spinal canal can lead to spinal cord injury and paralysis in crashes otherwise not causing injury in normal adults."[14]

- The duration of the collision peak or average vehicle acceleration is an incomplete measure of collision severity because of the delay between collision and occupant motion in low speed rear impacts.[15]

- "At the commonly used threshold for rear impacts of 8 km/h [i.e., 4.97 mph], the likelihood of showing any [injury] symptoms of any duration was 42.2%."[16]

- "In a low speed rear end impact, a vehicle has its speed abruptly increased. Interaction of seat and occupant causes unequal displacements of the upper body segments as the vehicle, seat and occupant are accelerated forward. Occupant head acceleration may not begin until the collision is over and the vehicle

12 "Automobile Bumper Behavior in Low Speed Impacts," D. King, G. Siegmund, M. Bailey, SAE Technical Paper 930211 (1993) doi:10.4271/930211, p.1.

13 "Automobile Bumper Behavior in Low Speed Impacts," D. King, G. Siegmund, M. Bailey, SAE Technical Paper 930211 (1993) doi:10.4271/930211, p.3.

14 "Serious Injury in Very-Low and Very-High Speed Rear Impacts," Davis C. Viano and Chantal S. Parenteau, ProBiomechanics, LLC (2008), SAE #2008-01-1485.

15 "Using Barrier Impact Data to Determine Speed Change in Aligned, Low Speed, Vehicle –to-Vehicle Collisions," SAE Technical Paper 960887 (1996) doi:10.4271/960887, p. 148.

16 "Injury Symptom Risk Curves for Occupants Involved in Rear End Low Speed Motor Vehicle Collisions," R. T. Moss, A. Bardas, M. Hughes and A. J. Happer, SAE Technical Paper 2005-01-0296 (2005) doi: 10.4271/2005-01-0296., p. 5. (2005).

has achieved its final velocity. Head acceleration can greatly exceed the vehicle acceleration."[17]

In addition to the Society of Automobile Engineers, a variety of other authors have published on this subject dating back to the 1980s with conclusions such as:

- The amount of damage to the automobile may bear little relationship to the forces applied to the cervical spine and to the injuries sustained by the cervical spine.[18]

- The amount of damage to the automobile bears little relation to the force applied to the cervical spine of the occupants. The acceleration of the occupant's head depends upon the force imparted, the moment of inertia of the struck vehicle and the amount of collapse of force dissemination by the crumpling of the vehicle.[19]

- The amount of damage sustained by the car bears little relationship to the force applied.[20]

- Each accident must be analyzed in its own right. Auto speed and damage are not reliable parameters.[21]

Finally, additional information supporting the reality of injury after "minor impacts" can be found by reviewing articles and books by Michael Freeman, PhD, MPD, DC and Attorney Karen Koehler. In fact, Dr. Freeman and Ms. Koehler have published a three volume work entitled *Litigating Minor Impact Soft Tissue Cases*, 2012–2013 ed. (AAJ Press) New Edition, that can be purchased online.[22]

17　"Automobile Bumper Behavior in Low Speed Impacts," D. King, G. Siegmund, M. Bailey, SAE Technical Paper 930211 (1993) doi:10.4271/930211, p.3.

18　"Whiplash Syndrome," Orthopedic Clinics of North America, by S. Hirsh, P. Hirsch, H. Hiramoto and A. Weiss (October 1988) 19(4), p. 791.

19　"Objective Findings for Diagnosis of Whiplash." Journal of Musculo-Skeletal Medicine, C. Caroll, P. McAfee, MD; L. Riley, Jr., MD (March 1986) / P 87 #4.

20　*The Spine*. Saunders, McNabb (1982), p. 648.

21　"Cervical Whiplash: Considerations in the Rehabilitation of Cervical Myofascial Injury," Ameis, Canadian Family Physician (September 1986).

22　http://store.westlaw.com/litigating-minor-impact-soft-tissue-cases-2012-2013-aaj-press/186873/40020421/productdetail.

As is clear from many of the references cited above, the lack of relationship between vehicle damage and bodily injury has been common knowledge for many years. Yet, as also discussed above, a very real prejudice still persists that often 1) prevents injured people from being adequately compensated, 2) prevents attorneys from accepting cases where there is low dollar property damage, and 3) prevents attorneys from winning injury cases involving low dollar property damage.

There are several ways to combat this prejudice. First, it is important for the attorney to be knowledgeable and armed with some of the scientific proof discussed above. Second, it is essential that the treating physicians and chiropractors know the science and are comfortable standing their ground when providing testimony. Third, once a lawsuit has been filed and it's clear that one of the insurance carrier's main defenses is lack of vehicle damage, it may be advisable to consider hiring a biomechanical engineer or, as David Ball suggests, a high school physics teacher.[23] It is the lawyer's job to figure out how to educate the jury and the public so that they can see the truth. Fortunately, the truth is on our side.

B. Delay in Onset of Pain or Symptoms

As stated in Chapter V, Section A, above, it is now well documented that there can be a delay after a wreck before symptoms from a whiplash-type injury begin to occur.[24]

---

23   David Ball on Damages 3, National Institutes for Trial Advocacy (2011) pp. 198–9.

24   National Institute of Neurological Disorders and Stroke, National Institutes of Health, Whiplash Information Page http://www.ninds.nih.gov/disorders/whiplash/whiplash.htm; *Humane Medicine Healthcare*, Volume 7 Number 3 (2007), by Robert Teasell, MD FRCPC, Glenn R. McCain, MD FRCPC, Harold Mersky, DM FRCPC, Hillel Finestone, MD CCFP FRCPC. P.2 http://www.humanehealthcare.com/Article.asp?art_id=330; *Whiplash Injuries: The Cervical Acceleration / Deceleration Syndrome*, Lippencott, Williams & Wilkins, by Stephen M. Foreman and Arthur C. Croft (2002), p. 359 ("It is not uncommon for pain to appear several days, and occasionally weeks, after the injury.") ; "Damage and/or Impact Absorber (Isolator) Movements Observed in Low Speed Crash Tests Involving Ford Escorts," R. Malmsbury, J. Eubanks, SAE Technical Paper 940912 (1994), doi:10.4271/940912, p.221.

However, as with the amount of damage to the vehicle, the insurance carriers are aware that not everyone knows the science. The carriers know that many people still believe that if you are injured in a wreck, you will know it immediately. Again, a common sense analogy, such as the weight lifting analogy discussed earlier, can be a good educational tool.

During and after a wreck, the body produces adrenaline and endocrine hormones that can also increase endorphin and cortisol levels. This response to the trauma of the wreck may override the body's pain mechanism.[25] Also, new studies show that a person's genetic makeup could also influence the amount of pain they feel after a wreck.[26]

While insurance adjusters still sometimes cling to the notion that everyone who is injured in a wreck must feel immediate pain, the vast majority of physicians and chiropractors are now aware of the fact that there is often a delayed pain reaction after a wreck. Emergency room instructions often say that the "patient has been instructed she may experience increasing pain and soreness over the next several days."

C. <u>Pre-existing Conditions (Degenerative Disc, Arthritis, etc.)</u>

In the framework of a personal injury claim, a "pre-existing condition" is something that you had before the wreck that is still present in your body at the time of the wreck, regardless of whether you knew it was there. The classic pre-existing condition (which we discussed earlier) is arthritis.

The law says that someone who causes a wreck 1) takes their victim as they find him or her and 2) is responsible for the aggravation of any pre-existing condition. So, if someone has arthritis in their neck, but

---

25 The Headington Institute: How Trauma Can Affect Your Body and Mind. http://www.headington-institute.org/Default.aspx?tabid=2073
26 "Pain Level After Car Crash Could Depend on Your Genes, Studies Say," by S. McLean, MD, J. Dumbrowski, MD, Medline Plus. A Service of the US National Library of Medicine, National Institutes of Health (October 16, 2012) http://www.nlm.nih.gov/medlineplus/news/fullstory_130329.html.

has never had neck pain, and is in a wreck and has a soft tissue neck injury that causes that arthritis to become symptomatic (i.e. aggravates that condition)—the person who caused the wreck is responsible for that pain and aggravation. Similarly, there may be a situation where someone had prior bouts of neck pain before the wreck and, therefore, knew they had arthritis. If they are then rear-ended and their neck begins to cause them problems, the person who caused the wreck is responsible for whatever aggravation of the condition he or she may have caused. The fact that the degree of aggravation in this example may be somewhat difficult to measure does not preclude someone from having a legal claim.

The issue of a pre-existing condition is often more of a perceived difficulty than a real difficulty. Aggravation of pre-existing conditions is now something that doctors believe can be a serious problem. Juries also seem to understand this situation and carriers will often ultimately acknowledge the problem once you prove to them that you understand the science and the law.

D. The "Invisibility" of the Injury

Another common "problem" in just about every soft tissue injury case is "the invisibility of the injury." This means that, unlike fractures, lacerations with scars and even herniated spinal discs—soft tissue injuries, by their very definition, are not visible of the naked eye. In fact, they are not visible to any kind of eye and cannot be seen on X-ray or MRI.

Despite the advances in technology over the years, even with newer tests such as MRIs and CT scans being used to look inside the body, there has still not been a generally accepted test that can view a soft tissue injury. Consequently, these cases often boil down to the injured person's word, and the word of his or her doctor, versus the adjuster, defense lawyer, or the defense expert.

Insurance companies, their attorneys and their expert witnesses, try to use the invisibility of the injury to create doubt in the mind of jurors and play on juror prejudices. It doesn't take much to bring this point out. For instance, a defense lawyer might ask the client's doctor,

"Well, she says it hurts there, and you are just taking her word for that, correct—because you have no objective evidence of any injury?"

The way to deal with the "invisibility" of a soft tissue injury is to have doctors who believe in and support the client's injury. It also helps greatly to have a credible client and to present the claim in an open and honest manner. Do not exaggerate.

E. Prior or Subsequent Injury

Having an injury or accident before a wreck or after a wreck is a much more difficult situation to deal with than simply having a pre-existing condition. All of the medical records relating to the other injury must be obtained. If the records indicate that the client had returned to pre-injury status before the wreck, then there should not be a huge issue. If the client was still being treated for the previous injury, then the client's doctor's opinion will be critical.

There are some situations where repeat injuries to the same part of the body can have a compounding effect. In these cases, an opinion from a medical provider regarding whether there is, in fact, a cumulative effect will be needed.

When unrelated injuries occur after a second wreck, the overall situation has to be examined. This includes in-depth discussions with the client and their doctors. The cause and effect of each wreck must be presented openly and honestly.

IX. WHAT TO EXPECT FROM YOUR ATTORNEY DURING THE COURSE OF YOUR SOFT TISSUE INJURY CASE

A. Intake and Initial Meeting

An attorney should talk to and/or meet with you before you hire them. There should be no fee for this meeting. This meeting and evaluation process is vitally important to the way the case is prepared. It's critical to have an experienced personal injury lawyer listen to and discuss your problems, desires, and expectations.

If the prospective client doesn't need an attorney then they should be given some free advice so that they can resolve the claim themselves.

If the law firm believes they can help a potential client and the person wants to hire the firm, it's important to obtain all of the necessary information as soon as possible. *There may be no time to waste in hiring investigators, taking photos, and making sure medical bills are paid in the correct fashion.*

The importance of an open and honest discussion with potential clients regarding their expectations and the process we plan to follow cannot be understated. Good personal injury attorneys do not promise things they cannot deliver or sugarcoat anything regarding the claims process. Nor is it fruitful or wise to attempt to predict the value of the client's case in the initial meeting. A good attorney needs much more information than is available at the first client meeting to advise his or her client regarding the value of the client's claim.

B. Letter of Representation

A "letter of representation" is the letter sent to the other driver's insurance company as soon as the attorney is hired. In fact, you should expect that letter to be faxed to the carrier within 48 hours of being hired.

This is a very important document for a couple of reasons. First, it notifies the insurance carrier that the law firm represents the client. Once the adjuster receives this letter, he or she is no longer permitted to have direct contact with the client. This is a relief for many clients who are being called at all hours of the day and being pestered by often-pushy adjusters to settle the case before the client even knows the extent of his or her injuries. Many companies will assign a new, higher-level adjuster to the claim after receiving a letter of representation. Some carriers have adjusters that deal only with claims where people are represented by an attorney.

Second, the letter of representation provides the carrier with a full description of the client's injuries and the extent of his or her current treatment. Insurance companies are bound by law to set funds aside as reserves for claims. If they believe the case involves only a very minor injury when, in fact, the client is hurt badly or may need surgery, the claim can become very difficult to resolve. Consequently, current information needs to be given to the carrier right away. It is always easier to settle a claim that has been reserved properly than one in which the reserves were set too low. Carriers cannot afford to have too many claims paid out at a higher level than the level at which the reserves are set.

C. Assisting and Advising the Client Regarding Medical Bill Payment

As discussed previously, the at-fault driver's insurance carrier will not pay for the injured person's medical treatment until the case is completely settled. Adjusters are, however, happy to leave the injured person with the *impression* that the bills are being paid because it may buy them weeks or months of peace. In other words, if the injury victim *believes* his or her bills are being paid, they won't constantly call the adjuster and hound him or her to make a payment. Often, it's not until the injured person begins to receive collection notices that they realize the adjuster has never paid a dime of the medical bills. Again, this plays right into the adjuster's hands by making the injury victim desperate for a quick settlement (at the adjuster's price) and completely dependent on the adjuster for salvation.

In Chapter VI, we discussed the different ways to pay for medical bills prior to resolving the case. As clients receive treatment, the law firm should assist and advise them on the best ways to pay for treatment, based on each client's circumstances. The lawyer's job is to assist and advise clients regarding all possible ways to pay medical bills so that they are not being pressured by bill collectors at a time when they should be focused on making a full recovery. The law firm should do everything permissible to make sure that clients receive the best possible medical care until their case can finally be resolved.

D. Assignment to a Paralegal

Shortly after a letter of representation is sent, most firms will assign the client's case to an experienced lead paralegal. This paralegal will work with the client throughout the case and talk to the client when the attorney is not available. They request medical records and bills, follow up on the requests, and monitor the manner in which the bills are paid. However, even an experienced personal injury paralegal is not a substitute for an experienced personal injury attorney. Therefore, an attorney should still monitor the case and make themselves available to talk to the client whenever necessary. You should expect to be able to talk to your attorney. You should also expect your phone calls to be returned.

E. Progression and Development of the Case

After a letter of representation is faxed out to the insurance adjuster, the file is set up and the information is put into the lawyer's computer system. Then the focus is on the client's treatment and how the medical bills can be paid (in full or in part) until the case is ready to be settled. The lawyer will determine what investigation needs to be done and will assign the case to one of their investigators.

If the client has health insurance, the law firm may contact the doctors and hospitals to make sure the client's bills are being turned in to health insurance. Similarly, the client's medical bills have to be obtained and submitted to the client's own auto insurance carrier for payment under the medical payments portion of the policy.

Also, if the client asks for assistance in finding the best doctors, chiropractors, osteopaths, or surgeons in his or her area, most law firms will try to help them get the best possible care. Unlike the doctors hired by many insurance carriers after a lawsuit is filed, the doctors recommended by good personal injury attorneys are not doctors that are professional evaluators who simply give helpful opinions to whoever pays them. The doctors recommended by good injury attorneys are medical providers known and trusted. They have track records of successfully helping people recover from their injuries. Clients may also need help finding doctors who are not prejudiced against those who have been injured in wrecks. Some family doctors and orthopedic surgeons will not see clients "because they were in a wreck." This is unconscionable.

As the client's medical treatment progresses, he or she should stay in touch with their lawyer's office on a continuous basis. The law firm wants to know what is happening with the client's treatment, whether he or she is improving and what the doctors and therapists are telling them. When they are released by their doctor(s), the law firm will request all of their medical bills and records and immediately begin preparing a settlement package to send to the insurance adjuster.

F. Medical Reports

Medical reports from treating doctors are a key element to any successful settlement package. This is also an area where people without attorney representation are at a clear disadvantage. Medical reports are necessary because, typically, medical records do not answer key legal questions in the case. Records are designed to memorialize the patient's condition, diagnosis, and the suggested treatment. They are not necessarily used by doctors to determine the cause of the patient's condition.[1]

---

1 Obviously, in some cases causation is important to determine diagnosis and treatment. This is not generally true, however, in soft tissue personal injury cases.

Even though all of the client's relevant medical records and bills will be sent to the insurance carrier, it is often necessary to ask the doctor for a separate report answering key questions. Often, lawyers will talk to doctors prior to asking for the report to get a better feel for the doctor's opinions and make sure the doctor knows what the legal requirements are for his answers. It's important that the doctor knows why the questions are being asked. The doctor's attention must be focused on issues the insurance carrier will want to have addressed.

Some of the important questions usually asked are as follows: 1) Was the client's condition a direct result of the wreck? 2) Was the treatment the client received reasonable, necessary, and a direct result of the wreck? 3) Do you believe the client will have any permanent problems as a result of this wreck?

Before answering these questions, it's important for the treating doctor to understand that the relevant standard in these cases is *not* "beyond a reasonable doubt." Every element of the case only must be proven by what is called a "preponderance of the evidence," which—in short—means more likely than not.

Beyond a reasonable doubt is the standard for judging criminal cases, not civil cases. Many medical questions simply cannot be answered beyond a reasonable doubt or with 100% certainty. Medical diagnosis and treatment often involves educated guess work and the process of elimination. Luckily, the law understands this. Since no one is going to jail in civil cases and because many civil questions cannot be answered with certainty, *certainty is not a requirement.*

Talking with the client's doctors, requesting reports, and obtaining the doctor's thoughts on the client's situation is also a great way to evaluate the case for potential litigation and trial. If the client's doctor is unfriendly, does not support the client, or refuses to become involved in the case, this is important to know *before* a lawsuit is filed.

Doctors who initially are uncooperative or resistant can often become very understanding and make good witnesses once they talk to an experienced attorney and learn more information about the situation. When they know that the client is being reasonable and only wants the truth, they often become more cooperative. A good lawyer will simply let these treating doctors know that they do not want them to stretch the truth or go out on a limb with their testimony. Instead, they just want honest responses based on the facts and the evidence. That should be every lawyer's approach to every case.

G. File Suit or Try to Resolve Without Filing?

In the majority of cases, an attempt to settle without filing a lawsuit will be made. At the very least, clients generally prefer to make an effort to resolve their claim before suit is filed. The reason is simple: it's much faster.

As Ray Bourhis said in *Insult to Injury,* "Our office always tries to settle cases, and the earlier the better... [w]ith the attendant lengthy discovery, procedural delays, trials, and appeals, most clients would rather eat red ants than litigate."[2] It simply takes longer to resolve a case once a lawsuit has been filed. It takes a long time to prepare the case for mediation, and even longer if the case goes to trial.

The days of filing suit and receiving a phone call from the defense lawyer a couple of weeks later with an increased settlement offer are long gone. When an attorney files a lawsuit, he or she should know that it's quite possible the case will go all the way to trial; however, the attorney also knows that there will probably be a mediation before trial, which allows at least one more opportunity to resolve the case.

Another reason to try to settle claims without filing a lawsuit is money. Litigating even a relatively small case can be very expensive. There are filing fees, deposition costs, numerous copies that must be made (after the insurance company requests 20 years of medical

---

2   *Insult to Injury, Ray Bourhis*, Berrett-Koehler Publishers, Inc., San Francisco (2005), at p. 27. This is a very good book dealing with insurance bad faith relating to disability policies.

records), and paying doctors for their time in preparing reports, meetings, or testimony. Once suit is filed, those costs become unavoidable.

There are, though, occasions when an attorney will file suit immediately without trying to settle the case. If the statute of limitations is close, then the case should be filed right away. If the client has serious injuries and it appears that the client will require lengthy treatment, then filing suit might be the best option. In this situation, filing suit may actually result in a faster resolution of the case. Instead of waiting a year or so for someone to finish treatment, only to find that the insurance carrier does not appreciate the gravity of the case, and then filing suit—filing suit immediately may result in a mediation 12–18 months later. The client's treatment will be completed by the time of the mediation and the case could resolve a full year earlier than it would have if the attorney had waited for treatment to end, tried to negotiate, and then filed suit. Significant cases involving severe injuries or death are also cases where the lawyer will likely suggest filing a lawsuit right away. Also, if a case requires the preservation of evidence, such as a semi-tractor trailer wreck, then a lawsuit should usually be filed immediately once an attorney is hired.

Insurance carriers are extra reluctant to part with significant dollars (i.e., hundreds of thousands or millions). They will try to hold on to the money as long as possible. Usually, they won't part with this type of money until they are looking down the barrel of an imminent trial date. After all, hanging on to millions of dollars and keeping it invested as long as possible is very advantageous for them.

H. The Settlement Package

1. What is a Settlement Package?

The settlement package consists of a detailed letter describing what happened to the client with attachments including the police report, medical records, medical reports, and medical bills. This package is sent to the insurance adjuster and asks him or her to evaluate the package and respond with a settlement offer.

The settlement package is by far the most important single item sent to an insurance carrier in every case where an out-of-court settlement is desirable. The settlement package is important for several reasons: 1) it contains everything the insurance company needs to make a decision on the claim and extend a settlement offer; 2) it organizes the entire case into one, easily manageable packet; and 3) it's a quick reference for the attorney in his or her discussions (i.e., arguments) with the insurance adjuster. A paralegal will make the lawyer a package that is identical to the package sent to the adjuster. Therefore, the adjuster and the lawyer can argue from the same reference point. The attorney can, for instance, tell the adjuster to "look at page four of the family doctor's records contained in tab two," when he or she wants to point something out to them. The adjuster can do the same with the lawyer.

2. What's in a Settlement Package?

A settlement package begins with a letter discussing how the wreck happened. The attorney will reference and attach the police report and discuss any important investigation discoveries made by the attorney. The lawyer normally concludes this section with an analysis of who is at fault and why. The next section of the letter discusses the injuries and treatment that the client incurred. The third section outlines all of the medical bills that resulted from the wreck. The next section discusses any income loss. The final section discusses the effects the wreck had on the client's life.

Attached to the letter are the police report, all of the client's medical records and bills, and a wage loss letter from the client's employer (if applicable). In a professional settlement package, everything is tabbed and indexed and in chronological order. The entire package is bound like a book or transmitted electronically.

3. Why Prepare a Settlement Package?

The settlement package should be complete and professional. This will impress the adjuster with the attorney's thoroughness and seriousness, while also telling the adjuster, in effect, "Here's everything you need to fully evaluate this claim; please do so immediately and get back to us with your response."

Without the benefit of an experienced personal injury attorney and a complete and professional settlement package, the adjuster is left to his or her own devices. *This is where many folks without an attorney find that their claim becomes bogged down.* If there is no lawyer to obtain and assemble all of the relevant information, the adjuster must do it on their own. If they do not, or if they do a poor job of it, the claim may never be settled because the adjuster's supervisor will not give them the authority to settle the claim. Or, the supervisor will give the adjuster inadequate authority due to the fact that the adjuster has not given the supervisor everything he or she needs to make a decision.

When an attorney handles an injury claim for a client, the client gives them a medical release so that the attorney can obtain the client's medical records and bills from the doctors and hospitals. These releases are necessary due to HIPPA and other privacy restrictions. The lawyer gathers all of the relevant information and then gives it to the insurance adjuster as described above.

If an injured person has no attorney and is attempting to negotiate the claim on their own, the only way the adjuster will work with them is if the injured person provides the adjuster with a medical release. *That puts the adjuster in complete control* (even more than they already were). You will not know which records and bills the adjuster has and which they do not. You will be totally dependent on the adjuster. They may tell you that they don't have a particular medical record that they need to complete your evaluation. You will not know if they have the record or not. In fact, you won't even know if they tried to obtain it. In short, you are at their mercy.

Moreover, there is something of an art to obtaining medical records in a timely manner. Good personal injury attorneys have people whose job is only to follow up on and obtain medical records as soon as the records are available. The adjuster, on the other hand, is in no hurry. He or she doesn't really care if it takes 30 days or 300 days for the doctor to copy and mail them your records. They may follow up, or they may not. The adjuster may even "lose" or "misplace" some of your records and have to re-request them.

Finally, people who do not have an attorney should look at the medical release the insurance adjuster gives them. What they will find is that the release is incredibly broad. Once you sign this document and give it to the adjuster, the adjuster will have the ability to obtain any of your medical records they desire (gynecological, psychological, etc.). The adjuster can also call your doctor and talk to them. This is dangerous because the adjuster can tell the doctor things about you and your claim that may not be 100% accurate. This can "poison" your own doctor against you and make him think you are claiming injuries or conditions that you are not claiming. The adjuster can threaten not to pay for treatment or testing that the doctor wants to do thereby discouraging the doctor from doing what is in your best interest. ***Never let an insurance adjuster talk to your doctor—ever.***

I. Following Up With the Carrier

Once a settlement package is sent out to the insurance adjuster, the lawyer must keep a close eye on the file and follow up with the adjuster to let them know that the lawyer is paying attention to how long it takes to hear back from them. This is *absolutely necessary*. Otherwise, a response may never be received.

As insurance companies continue to try to reduce expenses and squeeze more and more money out of their claims departments, adjusters have become more and more overloaded with files. Additionally, the bureaucratic levels the adjusters must go through to obtain settlement authority seem to be increasing. So overall, claims are taking longer to evaluate. Consequently, if you fail to follow up, your file seems to slip further and further toward the bottom of the pile.

Most good lawyers have a system of following up in writing and with phone calls that increase in intensity based on the length of time it takes to receive a response. The longer they go without hearing back, the more serious the follow-up communications become. Following up with insurance companies in writing is a necessity, since letters should make it into the file and can therefore be seen if a supervisor reviews the file or the file is later audited. Mere phone calls and voice mail messages must be manually entered into the file by the adjuster. If it is not in the adjuster's best interest to enter an angry voice mail from an injured person or an attorney into the file, the entry may not be made. It's much more difficult to make a letter disappear. Letters will remain a permanent part of the file for anyone reviewing the claim to see.

Sometimes, the lawyer may find it necessary to locate the adjuster's boss and send a copy of the correspondence to him or her. This kind of thing isn't necessarily easy for someone without an attorney to do. But, it's often necessary, and it often gets results!

J. Negotiating the Case

Once you receive a settlement offer from a carrier, the interesting part of the case begins. The lawyer will listen to the adjuster's analysis of the case. After the conversation concludes, the attorney should go back over the file and re-examine *everything*. Sometimes, adjusters point out flaws in the case that were already known. The adjusters may even bring up new things that were not previously known to the attorney. And sometimes, they just bring up the same mindless arguments.

Unfortunately, adjusters often tell folks without attorneys some of these alleged "problems" with their case and the folks listen. They then become worried or begin to feel guilty about some perceived "mistake" they made in their treatment regime. An experienced attorney, on the other hand, has heard these tired excuses from insurance adjusters literally thousands of times. A good and experienced personal injury lawyer will also have taken cases with the same "problems" to trial and gotten jury verdicts of many times what the adjuster is offering. That attorney will know, *from experience*, to take some of the things the adjuster says with a large grain of salt.

K. **Pre-Suit Mediation**

Remember, we're currently discussing how to prepare and resolve a soft tissue case without filing a lawsuit. While mediation is a common, and often mandatory, procedure after a lawsuit has been filed, it can also be helpful in certain cases *before* suit is filed.

A pre-suit mediation is usually a half-day meeting between the insurance carrier and the plaintiff's lawyer and his or her client. Everyone gets together under one roof to try to resolve the claim. Neither side can make the other do anything. The mediator is a neutral person agreed to by both sides. He or she has no power to make a determination on the case; they are simply a go-between who gives his or her thoughts and encouragement to each side.

A pre-suit mediation is suggested in soft tissue cases only where the injuries are complicated and the client has long-term problems. It is also important that the attorney believes the adjuster has a genuine interest in resolving the case for a reasonable amount of money. Obviously, the client must have reasonable expectations and a genuine interest in resolving the case. If those criteria have been met and the case does not seem to be lending itself to telephone negotiations, a pre-suit mediation may help get the case resolved.

X. <u>LITIGATION AND TRIAL OF A SOFT TISSUE PER-SONAL INJURY CASE</u>

A. <u>Considerations, Techniques and Philosophies</u>

First, filing a lawsuit is not necessarily the right thing to do in every soft tissue injury case. Most clients would rather have their attorney put together a settlement package and try to resolve the claim with the insurance adjuster first. Only when a reasonable settlement does not appear possible will the filing of a lawsuit need to be discussed.

Some clients mistakenly believe that filing a lawsuit is the magic solution that will somehow transform their claim and make the insurance carrier see things the way the client sees them. This is seldom the case. On the other hand, filing a lawsuit, even in what appears to be a difficult soft tissue case with moderate value, is not something to be afraid of. Often, carriers simply assume that attorneys will not be willing to take a soft tissue case all the way to trial. The only way to prove them wrong and gain their respect is to do it.

If you file a lawsuit, you should assume the case will eventually go to trial and *not* assume it will settle. It's a mistake to believe that insurance carriers won't litigate what they perceive to be small claims simply because they do not want to incur the defense lawyer's legal fees. Over the last 20 years, carriers have made a conscious effort to drastically reduce the attorney fees they pay. In some cases, they are even willing to pay their lawyers more to defend a case than they could pay to settle the case. For example, they may be willing to pay $10,000 in attorney fees and only offer $5,000 (i.e., spend $15,000) on a case that could have been settled for $9,000. In addition, many insurance companies now have their own lawyers who can defend cases and, therefore, do not have to hire an outside lawyer.

As Jay Feinman stated in *Delay, Deny, Defend*, "[t]he longer the company can drag it out, requiring the claimant to provide more and more information, to submit to onerous depositions, or simply to wait, the more likely it is that the claimant will give up and take a very small offer, or just go away."[1]

---

1   *Delay, Deny, Defend;* Jay M. Feinman, Portfolio (2010), p. 97.

The only way to counter this strategy is to prepare the case for a jury trial aggressively and to be willing to try the case if the carrier doesn't relent prior to trial.

The two main factors that influence people to settle personal injury cases (especially soft tissue cases) rather than go to trial are A) the length of time it takes to get a case to trial, and B) the additional expenses incurred once a lawsuit is filed. Unfortunately, personal injury lawyers do not have complete control over either of these factors.

It generally takes at least two years from the time a lawsuit is filed until a case can get to trial. Of course, the insurance carriers are in no hurry to pay a verdict, so the delay is just fine with them. Once again, it's the injured person who suffers while the case works its way through the system. This requires patience. The injury lawyer should do everything in his or her power to move the case as quickly as possible.

B. The Litigation Process

As part of a plan to pursue every lawsuit aggressively, an attorney will often file plenty of questions for the defense lawyers to answer and plenty of document requests asking them to turn over portions of their files early in the case. In legal jargon, these are "Interrogatories" and "Requests to Produce Documents."

Next, the attorney should schedule the defendant's deposition. Even in clear liability cases, it's important to meet and talk to the person who caused the wreck. It is important to know how that person will be viewed by the jury.

In Indiana and Ohio (as in most jurisdictions), the jury is never told that the defendant has automobile insurance to pay for the verdict. In fact, lawyers in these states are not really even permitted to discuss insurance. The lawsuit is filed against the person who caused the wreck—not the insurance company. Consequently, the personality of the defendant can be an important factor in the case.

The defense lawyers will ask to depose the injured person and his or her spouse. You should expect to be prepared by your lawyer for these encounters. By the time the deposition takes place, you should be comfortable with the process and the questions asked.

As mentioned above, once written questions and documents have been exchanged and the defendants and the injured person have been deposed, the case is ready for mediation. Mediation is simply a meeting between the attorneys, the insurance company representative, and the clients. The goal is to take another shot at settlement before both sides gear up and start spending serious money for trial. Mediations can also be helpful in determining whether there is any key piece of evidence that is missing. Sometimes, the insurance company will say that they need something they do not yet have, or that they would like one of the client's doctors to give his or her opinion on regarding a particular issue. In these situations, although the case may not be settled during the mediation, you can often make progress toward an eventual settlement. The defense lawyer's initial presentation in the mediation can also give clues as to what their approach will be at trial. It gives information regarding the perceived weaknesses of the plaintiff's case and allows the attorney time before trial to deal with these issues. Finally, if it appears that the case cannot be settled, the time at mediation can be spent preparing the client for trial and obtaining more information from the client that will be helpful at trial.

C. <u>Defense Doctors and Medical Examinations of the Client</u>

One of the key decisions the insurance company and their lawyer must make in each personal injury case where a lawsuit has been filed is whether to hire a doctor to give an opinion regarding the plaintiff's injuries and treatment. This is often referred to as an "Independent Medical Examination." *However, there is nothing independent about the process.* In soft tissue injury cases, insurance companies do not always hire their own doctor. Sometimes, they choose to simply attack the plaintiff's doctors. Whether this is a strategic decision or simply a budgetary consideration is often difficult to say.

When the defense does decide to hire a physician or chiropractor to testify in a case, they must make a strategic decision regarding the type of doctor they hire. They can hire a "regular," practicing physician or a professional file reviewer/testifier. If they chose the former, there is a much greater chance the exam will be favorable to the injured plaintiff.

In soft tissue cases, the doctors hired by insurance carriers often testify as follows: 1) the injured person suffered a (minor) soft tissue injury in the wreck; 2) soft tissue injuries get better within three to four months; 3) therefore, only medical treatment incurred within that time frame can be considered as related to the wreck; and 4) consequently, any pain or problems the injured person had after that time are not related to the wreck. The professional witnesses hired by the insurance industry assert these same four points in thousands of cases a year, regardless of whether there are facts to the contrary.

D. Trial

Once a soft tissue injury trial actually starts, it shouldn't take long to finish. The vast majority of soft tissue injury cases can be tried in two or three days. If the trial lasts longer than that, the injured person's attorney is probably taking far too much time to present his or her evidence.

Because the burden of proof is on the plaintiff (the injured person) in every personal injury case, it's up to that person's attorney to present all of the medical evidence documenting the client's injuries. The only way to do that is for the client's physicians, chiropractors, and therapists to testify. You are not allowed to simply put the medical records into evidence. Medical practitioners must be paid for their time, as must court reporters and videographers. These expenses add up and must be reimbursed out of the jury verdict.

As pointed out in Chapter VIII, soft tissue injury cases, by their very nature, have certain "difficulties." Trying soft tissue injury claims can be especially challenging when the case has multiple "difficulties." In other words, there are some cases that have all of the following: 1) a pre-existing condition, 2) low property damage, 3) a delay in onset of symptoms or pain after the wreck, 4) an invisible injury, and 5) a prior or subsequent injury. This host of issues often presents the greatest challenge to a personal injury attorney.

Generally, a good personal injury lawyer will combat all of these issues in the same way: 1) present the case in such a way that the jury will understand why the injured person has been forced to the courtroom and how fairly compensating that person is in society's best interest;[2] 2) address all issues head-on from the very beginning of the trial; 3) present short, simple, and straightforward testimony from the client's physician or chiropractor; 4) present very short testimony from "before and after witnesses" (i.e., plain folks who knew and spent time with the client before and after the wreck); 5) use analogies that connect with jurors; and 6) do not allow the defense lawyer to subtly imply that the client is faking or is untruthful without calling the lawyer onto the carpet and showing the jury that the lawyer doesn't have the courage to make this claim in open court in a straightforward manner.[3]

The bottom line is that soft tissue injury trials, more than any other type of personal injury trial, revolve around one thing—and only one thing—credibility. The injury is not visible and therefore the jury cannot "see" the problem independently. Consequently, the jury must rely on the truthfulness of the testimony presented. The entire trial is a process of gaining trust and letting the jury know that the lawyers and the injured person did not come to court to pull the wool over the jury's eyes. Instead, the injured person is there only to fairly and accurately present their case. The client should be fairly compensated and the jury should see that it is the defense—not the plaintiff—that is playing fast and loose with the facts, the science, and the rules. Fortunately, the truth is on your side. But, it is the personal injury lawyer's job to present the case in such a way that the jury is able to see the truth clearly.

---

2   See *Reptile, The 2009 Manual of the Plaintiff's Revolution,* by David Ball and Don C. Keenen (2009) Balloon Press, New York, NY,

3   See *Polarizing the Case (Exposing and Defeating the Malingering Myth),* by Rick Friedman, Trial Guides LLC (2007).

XI. <u>CONCLUSION</u>

Due to the changes made in the last 20 years by virtually every auto insurance carrier in the United States, handling soft tissue injury claims will continue to be a challenge, even for experienced lawyers. The fact that the carriers have actually targeted these claims for shrinkage, if not extinction, only adds to the challenge. Consequently, hardball tactics in every case will remain the norm—not the exception.

For the average person who attempts to handle a soft tissue injury claim without an attorney, the task is often insurmountable. Consequently, if you have been injured in a wreck, you are better off contacting an experienced personal injury attorney than attempting to handle the claim yourself. If your claim is too small or you make a quick and full recovery, a good lawyer will give you free advice and tell you there is no need to hire them. But you will never know his or her opinion unless you call and seek advice. The initial phone call should be free of charge—so you have nothing to lose.

Too often, soft tissue injuries that seem to be minor problems shortly after a wreck turn into chronic situations. By the time this happens, many folks have done things that have negatively and irreparably harmed their claims. Receiving competent treatment from experienced medical professionals and using all of the insurance coverages available to pay those medical bills can make all of the difference in the world.

So, if you've been injured in a wreck that was not your fault, you essentially have two choices: 1) you can sit back and let the insurance company do what it pleases; or, 2) you can seek professional assistance and let the carrier know that they cannot steamroll over you like a small lump in the asphalt.

If this were a perfect world, insurance companies would pay all claims quickly and fairly and I would be doing something else for a living. There would be no need to force them to adhere to their legal obligations. But, this is not a perfect world and insurance carriers want to make huge profits more than they want to help injured people. That's a fact. Once you come to grips with that fact, everything else makes sense.

Made in the USA
Las Vegas, NV
01 May 2024

89384032R00056